Preparing Instructional Objectives

A critical tool in the development of effective instruction

Revised Third Edition

Robert F. Mager

Mager Associates, Inc.
Carefree, AZ

Books by Robert F. Mager:

Preparing Instructional Objectives, Revised Third Edition*
Measuring Instructional Results, Revised Third Edition*
Analyzing Performance Problems, Revised Third Edition*
  (with Peter Pipe)
Goal Analysis, Revised Third Edition*
How to Turn Learners On ... without turning them off,
  Revised Third Edition*
Making Instruction Work, Revised Second Edition*
What Every Manager Should Know About Training,
  Second Edition
Troubleshooting the Troubleshooting Course
Life in The Pinball Machine, Second Edition

* Also sold as a six-volume set (The Mager Six-Pack)

Workshops by Robert F. Mager:

Criterion-Referenced Instruction (with Peter Pipe)
Instructional Module Development
The Training Director Workshop

Requests for permission to make copies of any part of this
publication should be mailed to:
  Mager Associates, Inc.
  P.O. Box 2180
  Carefree, AZ 85377

ISBN: 9781622091409
ISBN: 9781622091454 (Six-Volume Set)

Printed in the United States of America.

Contents

Note

Much of this book has been put together differently from most books you have read. On many pages you will be asked a question. When this happens, select the best answer, and then turn to the page referred to beside the answer. This way, you read only the material that applies to your needs, and you can proceed without being distracted by unnecessary explanations.

Another Note

Every once in a while you'll find some "boxed" material on a left-hand page. This is adjunct material that you may find interesting or useful. Read it as you go, or, if you find that distracting, save it for a rainy day.

Preface

Once upon a time a Sea Horse gathered up his seven pieces of eight and cantered out to find his fortune. Before he had traveled very far he met an Eel, who said,

"Psst. Hey, bud. Where ya' goin'?"

"I'm going out to find my fortune," replied the Sea Horse, proudly.

"You're in luck," said the Eel. "For four pieces of eight you can have this speedy flipper, and then you'll be able to get there a lot faster."

"Gee, that's swell," said the Sea Horse and paid the money, put on the flipper, and slithered off at twice the speed. Soon he came upon a Sponge, who said,

"Psst. Hey, bud. Where ya' goin'?"

"I'm going out to find my fortune," replied the Sea Horse.

"You're in luck," said the Sponge. "For a small fee I will let you have this jet-propelled scooter so that you will be able to travel a lot faster."

So the Sea Horse bought the scooter with his remaining money and went zooming through the sea five times as fast. Soon he came upon a Shark, who said,

"Psst. Hey, bud. Where ya' goin'?"

"I'm going to find my fortune," replied the Sea Horse.

"You're in luck. If you take this short cut," said the Shark, pointing to his open mouth, "you'll save yourself a lot of time."

"Gee, thanks," said the Sea Horse. He zoomed off into the interior of the Shark and was never heard from again.

The moral of this fable is that if you're not sure where you're going, you're liable to end up some place else.

It's true, isn't it? If you don't know where you're going, the best-made maps won't help you get there. Without a blueprint, the finest materials and the most skilled artisans wouldn't be able to create the house of your dreams. Similarly, without a way to communicate your instructional objectives to others:

- You wouldn't be able to decide which instructional content and procedures would help you to accomplish your objectives.
- You wouldn't be able to create measuring instruments (tests) that tell you whether your students had become competent enough to move on.
- And your students wouldn't be able to decide for themselves when to stop practicing.

A clear statement of objectives, on the other hand, will help you avoid these and other problems, because they will give you, and others, a sound basis for selecting instructional content and procedures, as well as the means for finding out whether your important outcomes have actually been accomplished. Objectives will also provide you with a communication tool through which you can let others know what you, or someone else, has decided is worth teaching.

This book is about the characteristics of usefully stated objectives. It will show you how to draft objectives that communicate your instructional intent, and it will show you where objectives fit in the larger scheme of the instructional enterprise.

This book is NOT about who should select objectives, nor is it about how one goes about deciding what is worth teaching. These are critical issues, but they are beyond the scope of this book.

Specifically, the objective of this book is this:

Given any objective in a subject area with which you are familiar, be able to identify (label) correctly the *performance*, the *conditions*, and the *criteria* of acceptable performance when those characteristics are present.

Once you recognize the presence or absence of the characteristics of well-stated objectives, you will be able to prepare your own.

If you care about developing and/or delivering instruction that will give your students the skills and knowledge important for them to have, this book is for you.

Robert F. Mager
Carefree, Arizona

1
Objectives

Instruction is effective to the degree that it succeeds in:

- changing students
- in desired directions
- and not in undesired directions.

Instruction that doesn't change anyone has no effect, no power. If it changes students in undesired directions (that is, if it has unwanted side effects), it isn't called effective; instead, it is called poor, undesirable, or even harmful instruction. Instruction is successful, or effective, to the degree that it accomplishes what it sets out to accomplish.

Once you decide to teach someone something, several kinds of activity are required if your instruction is to be successful. For one thing, you must assure yourself that there is a need for the instruction, making certain that (1) your students don't already know what you intend to teach and (2) instruction is the best means for bringing about the desired change. For another, you must clearly specify the outcomes or objectives you intend your instruction to accomplish. You must then select and arrange learning experiences for your students in accordance with the principles of learning and must evaluate student performance according to the objectives originally selected. In other words, first you decide where you want to go, then you create and administer the means of getting there, and then you arrange to find out whether you arrived.

The steps for accomplishing this arrange themselves into these four main phases:

Analysis

Design/development

Implementation

Evaluation/improvement

A number of procedures and techniques are available through which to complete them. The analysis phase, for example, should answer questions such as these:

Is there a problem worth solving?

Is instruction a relevant part of the solution?

If so, what should the instruction accomplish?

After all, instruction is only one of several possible solutions to problems of human performance. Unless a suitable analysis is performed before instruction is developed, it is quite possible to construct a magnificent course that doesn't help anybody at all. It is possible to construct a course that nobody needs, either because instruction is unrelated to solving the problem that gave rise to it or because it "teaches" things the students already know. Techniques such as performance analysis[1] and goal analysis[2] can help avoid such wasteful practices.

[1] See *Analyzing Performance Problems,* Third Edition, R. F. Mager and Peter Pipe (1997).
[2] See *Goal Analysis,* Third Edition, R. F. Mager (1997).

If analysis reveals that instruction is needed, objectives are drafted that describe the important outcomes intended to be accomplished by that instruction. In other words, objectives are drafted that answer the question "What is worth teaching?" Instruments (tests) by which the success of the instruction can be assessed are then drafted.

Only after the preceding steps have been completed is the actual instruction drafted, tested, revised, and then put into use. And, please note, only after the analysis phase is complete or near completion are objectives drafted. This is an important point, because when you read or hear that "the first thing you do is write objectives" or "objectives are written before instruction is designed," you should translate that into "*after* the analysis is completed, then objectives are prepared *before* the instruction is designed."

What Is an Instructional Objective?

An instructional objective is a collection of words and/or pictures and diagrams intended to let others know what you intend for your students to achieve.

- It is related to intended outcomes, rather than the process for achieving those outcomes.
- It is specific and measurable, rather than broad and intangible.
- It is concerned with students, not teachers.

The Objective of This Book

This book is concerned with the *characteristics* of a usefully stated objective, rather than with its derivation or selection. The purpose of the book is limited to helping you specify and communicate those instructional intents you or someone else has decided are worth achieving. If this book achieves its objective, you will be able to recognize the characteristics of well-stated objectives when they are present. Once you can recognize desirable characteristics, and after a bit of practice, you will be able to prepare your own objectives by modifying your drafts until they are well stated.

Specifically:

*Given any objective in a subject area with which you are familiar, be able to identify (label) correctly the **performance**, the **conditions**, and the **criteria** of acceptable performance when those characteristics are present.*

To help you reach this objective, I will describe some of the advantages to be gained from the careful specification of objectives, describe and illustrate the characteristics of a usefully stated objective, and give you some practice in recognizing such objectives. At the end, you will have an opportunity to determine just how well our efforts have succeeded.

Before we begin, it will be useful to look in some detail at the difference between instructional process and instructional results.

Outcomes vs. Process

An objective is related to an intended outcome of instruction, rather than the process of instruction. For example, when a chef adds seasoning to a soup, that is part of the process of cooking. But it isn't the result of the cooking. The soup itself is the outcome, or result, of the cooking.

Lecturing is something an instructor does to help the students to learn; it is part of the process of instruction. But a lecture is not the purpose of the instruction. The purpose of instruction is to facilitate learning. So when teachers teach (process), they do it because they hope that students will learn (the result or outcome). Therefore, statements such as the following are descriptions of instructional process, rather than of intended results.

- To provide a lecture series on phrenolationism.
- Be able to perform well in a role-play situation.
- This course provides extensive practice exercises.

Because recognizing the difference between process statements and outcome statements is critical to the effective use of objectives, it will be useful to check your ability to spot the difference. Following are two statements. Turn to the page number shown beside the outcome statement.

Be able to sing.   *Turn to page 9.*

Develop confidence.   *Turn to page 7.*

Uh, oh. What are you doing here? Nowhere in this book are you directed to this page.

In this kind of book, when you are asked a question, you are to select what you think is the correct response, and then turn to the page number indicated beside that alternative.

You see, I'm trying to tailor my comments to your needs so that you won't have to waste your time reading about things you already know. By answering the periodic questions, you'll be able to test yourself through the book a lot faster than if you had to read all the pages.

Don't miss this note!

> Every once in a while you'll find some material boxed on a left-hand page. This is adjunct material that you may find interesting or useful. Read it as you go, or, if you find that distracting, save it for a rainy day.

Please return to the page from whence you cometh.

You said that "Develop confidence" is an outcome statement.

Let me try again. Think of your instruction as being like a train that takes your students from one place to another. The question to be answered by an objective is, "What are students expected to be like when they arrive at their destination?"

It might help to think of the difference between statements describing the process of building a house and those describing the characteristics (outcomes) of a completed house. For example, here are some process statements about the construction process:

- The foundation is laid before the walls go up.
- Walls are to be constructed of crushed tin cans.
- Scaffolding will be used when installing the roof.

In contrast, the following statements describe characteristics (outcomes) of the completed house:

- The house contains three fireplaces.
- The front of the house faces south.
- All windows are constructed of double-pane glass.

Outcomes are the results we get from processes.

Turn to page 5 and select the correct response.

Right on! "Be able to sing" is an outcome statement. It describes something we might want our students to be able to do. Keep this up and you'll fall out of the back of the book in no time.

Specific vs. General

Another characteristic of an objective is that it is specific, rather than general, broad, or "fuzzy." If objectives are fuzzy, they don't do us any good and we might as well not bother with them. We want them to be specific, so they will help us to make good instructional decisions.

Here are a few examples of specific and fuzzy statements. Put a check mark beside the specific statements, and then turn the page to check your responses.

Understand logic.	_____
Know your enemy.	_____
Thread this needle.	____✓____
Reassemble this cat.	____✓____
Think.	_____
Smile when addressing a customer.	____✓____

Turn the page to check your responses.

The items checked are specific; the others are fuzzy.

Understand logic.	_____
Know your enemy.	_____
Thread this needle.	✓ _____
Reassemble this cat.	✓ _____
Think.	_____
Smile when addressing a customer.	✓ _____

As you will see, specific statements are precise; you can immediately determine whether or not you have met the objective. If you have not met it, the specific statement indicates what you must do to meet it. On the other hand, general or abstract statements (fuzzies) leave you in the dark. They must be reworded until they say exactly what is expected.

Measurable vs. Unmeasurable

△ An objective is considered measurable when it describes a tangible outcome. For example, objectives that describe intended outcomes that you can see or hear are measurable.

For example, an objective that says, "Be able to tie a knot," is measurable, because we can see knot-tying behavior and therefore assess whether it meets our expectations.

On the other hand, a statement that says, "Be able to internalize a growing awareness of confidence," is not only not measurable, it can't even be called an objective. What would you measure? What would you watch a student do to decide whether or not the internalizing had occurred to your satisfaction? The statement doesn't say.

Students vs. Instructors

"Instructional" objectives describe the student's performance rather than the instructor's performance. Objectives that describe the instructor's performance are called "administrative" objectives. Instructors help students to accomplish the instructional objectives.

For example, some of the following statements relate to what instructors might do, and some relate to what students might be expected to learn to do. Put a mark beside those that relate to student performance.

_____ Lecture on the theory of tail wagging.

___✓___ Be able to draw a duck.

_____ Arrange field trips.

_____ Arrange role-playing exercises.

___✓___ Be able to write a business letter.

___✓___ Explain the importance of the bottom line.

___✓___ Be able to make change without error.

Turn to page 12.

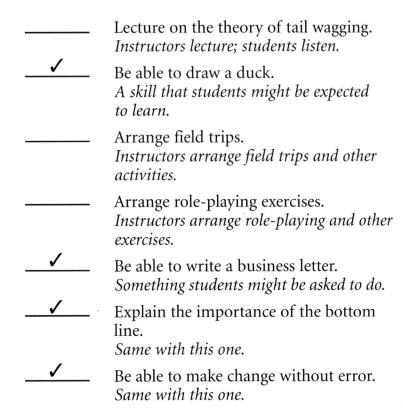

—————   Lecture on the theory of tail wagging.
Instructors lecture; students listen.

✓ —————   Be able to draw a duck.
A skill that students might be expected to learn.

—————   Arrange field trips.
Instructors arrange field trips and other activities.

—————   Arrange role-playing exercises.
Instructors arrange role-playing and other exercises.

✓ —————   Be able to write a business letter.
Something students might be asked to do.

✓ —————   Explain the importance of the bottom line.
Same with this one.

✓ —————   Be able to make change without error.
Same with this one.

This might have seemed like a trivial exercise, yet there are many instructors who cannot yet distinguish between statements about *instructor* activity and *student* performance. (If you're unlucky, you'll run into hundreds of so-called "objectives" that begin something like, "Seventy percent of the class must be able to _____." Such statements relate to teacher goals, not intended student outcomes.)

For now it's enough to know that if an objective is going to be useful, it needs to contain *specific and measurable student outcomes*.

2
Why Care About Objectives?

To wonder why we should care about instructional objectives is like wondering why we should know:

- where we're going before buying a bus ticket
- what we're intending to manufacture before turning on the factory
- whom we intend to hit before throwing the pie

After all, instruction is only successful to the degree that it succeeds in changing students in desired ways, rather than in undesired ways. If instruction doesn't change anyone in desired ways, it isn't any good, regardless of how elegant the lectures are or how complicated the hardware used to present it is.

Simply, if instruction is to accomplish desired outcomes, it is imperative that those designing the instruction, as well as the ones doing the instruction, have a clear picture of those desired outcomes.

Because objectives are tools for describing intended outcomes, they provide a key component for making instruction successful and are useful in several ways.

Materials/Procedure Selection

When clearly defined objectives are lacking, there is no sound basis for the selection of instructional materials and procedures. If you don't know where you're going, how will you know which road to take to get there? (Or, as Yogi Berra said, "When you reach a fork in the road, take it!")

After all, machinists and surgeons don't select tools until they know what they're intending to accomplish. Composers don't orchestrate scores until they know what effects they are trying to create. Too often, however, one hears instructors arguing the relative merits of books versus lectures, computers versus video, self-pacing versus group-pacing—without ever specifying just what results they expect these things to achieve. Instructors simply function in a fog of their own making unless they know what they want their students to accomplish as a result of their instruction.

Instructor Ingenuity

Once the important outcomes of instruction have been derived and clearly stated, it is then possible to say to instructors, "Here are the objectives you are expected to achieve. Now go use your best wisdom, experience, and ingenuity to achieve them." In other words, the existence of the objectives can free instructors to be creative and flexible.

With objectives in place, it is no longer necessary to expect all instructors to be doing the same thing at the same time during a lesson. It's like a football game, where the quarterback selects the best play to get his team where he knows it has to go. You can imagine what a game would be like if all quarterbacks had to use the same sequence of plays and have to succeed or fail "merely" on the basis of how well each play was executed.

Consistent Results

Objectives provide the basis for achieving consistent instructional results. With the instructional goal posts clearly visible, it is possible to provide enough instruction and practice so that all students learn to perform at least as well as the objectives require. Some will learn more or reach a higher performance level than the objectives require, of course, but everyone can be expected at least to accomplish each objective.

With objectives, it is possible to achieve desired results without requiring consistency in the process for getting those results.

Measurable Results

How many courses have you taken in which the tests had little or nothing to do with the substance of the instruction? No surprise there. Unless objectives are clearly and firmly fixed in the minds of both instructors and students, tests are likely to be at best misleading; at worst, they will be irrelevant, unfair, or uninformative. Without clear objectives it simply isn't possible to decide which measuring instrument will tell you what you want to know.

She: Why are you waving that meter stick around?

He: I wanna know how windy it is.

Clearly stated objectives provide a sound basis for selecting the means by which to find out whether they have been achieved. Suppose part of an objective said, "Be able to make a low-altitude parachute jump . . . " How could you find out whether your students can actually do what they were supposed to learn to do? How about a multiple-choice test? After all, they're easy to score, and you could even claim to be using an "objective" test. No? What about something in a true-false variety? You could have lots of fun dreaming up wrong answers.

True/false: Parachutes always come in pairs.

True/false: Red parachutes are heavier than white ones.

How about an essay test? Students should be able to describe how a parachute works and how they are packed, shouldn't they?

No doubt you saw right off that the only way to test whether someone can make a low-altitude jump is, in effect, to say, "Lemme see you make a low-altitude jump." And how did you know that? Because the objective clearly stated the intended outcome of the instruction. With clear objectives you don't have to be an expert in test construction to select and create measuring instruments that will tell you whether your objectives have been accomplished.

Goal Posts for Students

Clearly defined objectives also can be used to provide students with the means to organize their own time and efforts toward accomplishment of those objectives. When the instructional intent has been clarified—and revealed to the students—it is no longer necessary for them to guess what an instructor might have in mind for them to accomplish.

He: Think we should memorize the chapters?

She: Don't bother. This one's a footnote fanatic.

As you know too well, many students are required to spend considerable time and effort learning the peculiarities of their instructors when those instructors fail or refuse to let them in on the secret of what they're expected to learn. Unfortunately, such knowledge can be useful in helping students breeze through a course with little more than a bagful of tricks designed to rub the instructor the right way. Clear objectives in the hands of the students eliminate the need for such time-wasting and anxiety-producing activity.

Which leads to the final point: With clear objectives, it is possible to organize the instruction itself so that instructors and students alike can focus their efforts on bridging the gap between (a) what each student can already do and (b) what each needs to be able to do to accomplish each of the assigned objectives.

Instructional Efficiency

We have seen time and time again that when good objectives have been derived, existing instruction often can be drastically shortened. In fact, instruction can sometimes be eliminated altogether when the objectives help reveal that inadequate job performance is due to factors other than lack of knowledge or skill.

This "miracle" is effected by comparing information about what people need to be able to do (as described by the objectives) with information about what they already know how to do (as provided by target-population descriptions and/or performance tests). When there is no difference between the "should be able to do" and "can already do," it is clear that more instruction won't help; it is clear that the source of inadequate performance must be found elsewhere. (There are many reasons why people don't do what they already know how to do: Unclear performance expectations; absence of tools, space, or authority to perform as expected; and so on.)

Objectives are also useful in helping organizations respond to the pressures of downsizing and the resulting need to do more with less. With such pressures operating, it is critical for workers to become competent as quickly as possible. At the

Here is an example of how, when objectives aren't stated carefully, activities in the classroom can hinder the student's efforts to achieve an objective.

At a large training establishment operated by the government, a course was once offered in which students were to learn how to operate and repair a big, complex electronic system. The goal of the course was simply stated: To be able to operate and maintain the *XYZ Electronic System.*

Since it was impossible (because of the exorbitant cost) to provide each student with a separate system to practice on, it was decided to increase the amount of troubleshooting students did during the course by giving them some "practice" in the classroom as well as in the laboratory.

During the classroom troubleshooting exercises, the instructor would pose various problems for the students to solve. He would point out a component on one of the many schematic diagrams of the equipment and ask, "What would happen if this component were bad?" Students would then trace through the circuitry (on paper) in an effort to divine the *symptoms* that would appear as a result of the instructor's hypothetical trouble. The students, in other words, were given a trouble and asked to induce symptoms.

This procedure, however, was exactly opposite to that which was expected of the learners on the final examination or on the job. There they were typically shown a *symptom* and asked to locate the *trouble.* The instructors were expecting learners to run forward by teaching them how to run backward.

Thus, for want of a specific statement of objectives, students were not only learning the wrong thing, but the habits they were developing in the classroom were in conflict with those they were expected to use on the job.

same time, it is important that they not be removed from their job sites any longer than absolutely necessary to attend training. Objectives not only allow the training to be streamlined to the needs of the individual trainee, they often allow instruction to be delivered a module at a time, at more convenient locations, and during short periods that do not disrupt the flow of work.

Summary

Objectives are useful for providing:

- A sound basis for selection of instructional materials and procedures,
- Room for instructor creativity and ingenuity,
- Measurable instructional results,
- Tools for guiding student efforts, and
- A basis for realizing instructional efficiency.

There are additional advantages, not the least of which is that the act of drafting objectives causes one to think seriously and deeply about what is worth teaching. When objectives are drafted for courses already in existence, they can serve to spotlight opportunities for instructional improvement.

A Basic Distinction

Before practicing to recognize the characteristics of a usefully stated objective, we should make sure we're beating on the same drum. So far, we've noted that objectives are statements describing intended instructional outcomes, rather than the processes or content that will be used to achieve those outcomes. They describe ends rather than means. Therefore, there is a significant difference between course descriptions and their intended outcomes.

Course descriptions tell what a course is about, e.g., "Includes study of all the great philosophers, from Aristotle to Berra."

Objectives describe what students are expected to be able to do, e.g., "Given a stick, be able to beat a dead horse to oblivion."

Now read the following statement and the questions at the end of the statement. Then turn to the page number shown beside your answer to those questions.

A general survey of the organizing and administration of elementary- and secondary-school libraries, with emphasis on methods of developing the library as an integral part of the school. Includes functions, organization, services, equipment, and materials.

What does the above statement represent? Is the statement an *objective* of a course or a *description* of a course?

An objective of a course.   **Turn to page 23.**

A description of a course.   **Turn to page 27.**

Some years ago, the chief instructor of a 32-week military course noticed the peculiar fact that students were doing rather poorly on every *third* examination. Scores were low on the first exam and then considerably better on the next two, low on the fourth and high on the next two, and so on. Since scores were consistently low and then high even for the brighter students, the instructor correctly concluded that this peculiarity was not because of student intelligence or the lack of it. He then decided that he was so close to the course he probably wasn't seeing the woods for the trees, so he called in consultants.

During their analysis of the situation, the consultants noticed that the course was divided into five sub-courses. Each sub-course was taught by a different team of instructors, and during each sub-course the students were given three examinations. They discovered that students did poorly on the first test because they hadn't been told what to expect; they had to use the first test as a means of finding out what the instructors expected. Once they had learned what the objectives were, they did much better on the next two exams of that sub-course. But then another team of instructors took over. Believing the second team's examinations would be similar to those of the first team, the students prepared themselves accordingly, only to discover that the rules had been changed *without their knowledge.* They then did poorly on the fourth test (the first test given by the new instructor team). And so it went throughout the course. Objectives were vague, and the students were never told what to expect.

Once these conditions were made known to the chief instructor, the problem was easily solved.

You said the statement was an objective of a course. Apparently I didn't make myself clear earlier, so let me try again.

A course *description* tells you something about the content and procedures of a course. A course *objective* describes a desired outcome of a course.

Perhaps the sketch below will help make the distinction clear:

INSTRUCTION
(course)

PREREQUISITES	DESCRIPTION	OBJECTIVES
What a learner has to be able to do to qualify for a course.	What the course is about.	What a successful learner will be able to do at the end of the course.

Whereas an objective tells what the learner will be able to do as a result of some learning experiences, the course description tells only what the course is about.

The distinction is quite important, because a course description does not explain what will be accepted as adequate accomplishment. Though a course description might tell students which field they will be playing on, it doesn't tell them where the boundary lines are, where the goal posts are located, or how they will know when they have scored.

It is useful to be able to recognize the difference between an objective and a description, so try another example.

Which of the following statements looks most like an objective?

In at least two computer languages, be able to write and test a program to calculate arithmetic means.

Turn to page 29.

Discusses and illustrates principles and techniques of computer programming.

Turn to page 31.

*College catalogs frequently mislabel the content.
For example,*

Course Objective: To cover the military strategies
and tactics of the Civil War.

*Statements such as these may say something about the
objective of the instructors, but nothing about what the
students should be able to do at the conclusion of the course.
Calling it an objective doesn't make it one.*

You said the statement was a description of a course. And right you are! I'm sure you recognized the statement as a course description lifted from a college catalog.

One final word about course descriptions before moving on. Though a description sometimes tells us a good deal about what a course includes, it does not tell us what the course is supposed to accomplish. More important, it does not tell us how to determine when the intended outcomes have been achieved.

So, though a course description may be perfectly legitimate for a catalog, here we are interested *only* in the intended *results* of that course.

Zip ahead to page 33.

You said "In at least two computer languages, be able to write and test a program to calculate arithmetic means" was a statement of an objective.

Correct! The statement describes an intended outcome—something the student is expected to be able to do—rather than the procedure by which the student will develop that skill.

Since you can tell the difference between a course description and a course outcome, it's time to move on.

Turn to page 33.

Well . . . no. The collection of words that led you to this page is a piece of a course description—and not a very good description, at that. Look at it again:

Discusses and illustrates principles and techniques of computer programming.

Notice that the statement seems to be talking about what the course covers or what the instructor will be doing. There isn't a word about what the student will be able to do as a result of the instruction. I hope you are not being misled by the fact that college catalogs are full of statements like this one. They are not statements of learning outcomes, and they are not what we are concerned with here.

Let me try to explain the difference this way. A course description outlines various aspects of a *process* known as instruction. A course objective, on the other hand, is a description of the intended *results* of the instructional process. It's sort of like the difference between bread and baking. Baking is what you do to get the bread, but it isn't the same as bread. Baking is the process; bread is the result. Similarly, instruction is the process; student competence is the result.

Turn to page 5 and read the material again.

3
Where Objectives Come From

Instructional objectives come from many sources. Some of these sources are rational, systematic, and useful; others are egocentric, disorganized, and astonishingly haphazard. Systematic derivation procedures lead to objectives truly worth accomplishing. The "I know what's best for students" approach, on the other hand, often leads to objectives that describe outcomes of little value to the student. This is because "I know best" decisions can so often be totally disconnected from any real need for instruction. Such questionable decisions can be derived from prior experience which may be out of date, from biases inspired by the chapters that happen to be included in a textbook, from instructor preferences about what they *like* to teach, or from inertia—"I've *always* taught it this way."

When derived from any of these non-systematic "methods," the resulting instruction can prove totally useless to the student, regardless of the importance of the subject matter to the instructor. Unfortunately, people embedded in the middle of an educational system can easily lose sight of the fact that good objectives are ultimately derived from the real world. (That's another way of saying that the purpose of instruction is to help someone learn to do something of value—to someone other than the instructor.) Instructors can get so engrossed in "teaching points" that they forget that the purpose of the enterprise is to get beyond the "talk about" to the "DO about."

Properly derived objectives—all genuine objectives—are ultimately about *doing.* They describe the desired results of instruction, rather than the activities of instruction. They provide descriptions of instructional destinations, thus allowing us to derive components of the instructional process that will be truly relevant to reaching those desirable destinations.

Most instructional objectives are derived from two general sources:

1. Personal desires
2. External needs

Personal Desires

People often decide that they want to accomplish something on their own, with or without formal instruction. New Year's resolutions, for example, often describe personally selected objectives:

"I will lose ten pounds by June 1."

"I will be out of debt by the end of this year."

Self-selected goals that involve *learning* might include the following:

"I'll learn to play the harp so that I can wow my neighbors at the block party next month."

"My spouse is leaving me, so I'm going to the bookstore to learn everything I can about how to handle a divorce."

"My boss returned my monthly report with all the spelling errors circled. I'd better learn how to spel."

Having decided, they are the ones who must take action to accomplish their goals. Those who prefer a systematic approach will take steps to decide as precisely as they can just what it is they hope to accomplish through their learning. They will, in other words, establish a list of objectives. Having done that, they are in a much better position to decide what actions they need to take to accomplish them.

External Needs

Suppose, though, that you have decided to become a licensed Zamboni driver, so that you can get paid for tooling around an ice rink while waving at the cheering throngs. In this instance, it doesn't matter much what you may want to learn, because the learning need will be defined by what it takes to accomplish the task. In other words, the instructional objectives for your learning will be derived not from your personal preferences, but from what other people have determined to be the tasks that any Zamboni driver has to be able to perform.

If you sign up for instruction, the objectives will be derived and established by the coach or instructor. But how do they derive these and other objectives? They do it by analyzing various levels of needs. The analysis might begin by reviewing the needs of an entire organization, or it might begin at a lower level, such as a division or department. At the end of the process, the analysis finally reveals needs that must be fulfilled if the desired goals are to be achieved. "Need" here refers to a performance "hole" that must be filled if an expected or planned accomplishment is to be realized. For example:

> "To qualify for enrollment in Algebra II, students need to be able to perform these tasks." (List would be added here.)

Because traditionally most instruction has been done in classrooms, we sometimes forget that we often use those very same classrooms for things other than instruction. For example, here are the kinds of activities for which classrooms are often used:

Information sessions:	"Let me explain the benefits package."
Sales sessions:	"Let's begin by singing the company song."
Motivation sessions:	"You really oughta wanna get out and sell."
Orientation sessions:	"Here's an overview of this course."
Bull sessions:	"Let's knock some new-product ideas around."
Instructional sessions:	"Here's how to do it."

Notice that only the instructional sessions tend to change behavior in carefully specified ways. Therefore, instructional objectives are appropriate only for teaching sessions. The fact that "it" is done in a classroom shouldn't stampede you into deriving and drafting objectives. Create objectives only when there are things that people don't yet know how to do and also need to know how to do.

"To perform your job competently, you need to be able to solder well enough to meet military specifications."

"An analysis reveals that 50% of our sales force can't speak English well enough to communicate with our customers. We need to correct this problem as soon as possible."

"We're planning to make significant changes in the organization, and people will need to have these listed skills and knowledge to function successfully." (List would be added here.)

Once these performance needs have been derived, they are compared against what individuals can and cannot now do. Those things that people cannot now do, *and* need to be able to do, become objectives for instruction.

Systematic Derivation of Instructional Objectives

Those responsible for meeting external performance needs (e.g., performance analysts, instructional developers) use a systematic procedure to derive objectives and to decide what is worth teaching. This procedure follows some version of the following steps:

1. *Task listing.* Any job, position, profession, or hobby consists of a collection of tasks. This collection names the things that people do when carrying out their work or play. (Note: A task is a series of steps leading to a useful/meaningful outcome.) Here are the names of some tasks that people might have to perform:

Here is an example of a skill hierarchy, or pyramid, showing the relationships between the skills involved in making a pizza.[1]

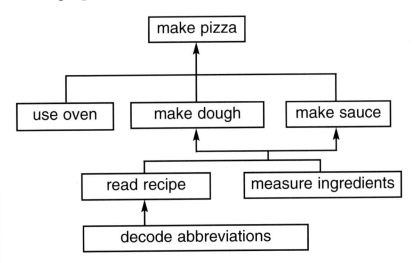

Read the hierarchy this way: Before students can practice the main skill (making pizza), they need to be able to use an oven, make dough, and make sauce. These skills are subordinate (prerequisite) to the terminal skill in that they must all be learned before the terminal skill can be practiced in its entirety. But these three skills are independent of one another; *they can be learned in any order.*

Before the skills of making dough or making sauce can be practiced, students will have to be able to read a recipe and measure ingredients. These skills are both subordinate to the sauce-and-dough making but are independent of one another. Either could be learned first. Finally, to read a recipe, the learner first has to learn how to decode abbreviations.

---

[1] Hierarchy courtesy of Diane Pope.

- Prepare a lesson plan
- Take spinal X-rays
- Change a tire
- Interview an applicant
- Write a report
- Write correctly spelled letters
- Play a song
- Send/receive Morse code
- Drive a golf ball at least 200 yards

If the job is new, or if there is some question about whether the current tasks being performed are appropriate, a "higher" level of analysis will be indicated. In other words, first we'll decide what the job should consist of, and then we'll list the tasks that will be required to do the job.

2. *Task analysis.* Once the tasks have been identified, the next step is to draw a picture for each task describing the steps and key decisions that make up the task. This procedure, called task analysis, reveals the components of the task by describing what a competent person does when performing the task. It gives the reason for starting to perform the task; it describes the steps followed and decisions made during completion of the task; and it indicates how to tell when the task has been completed, i.e., when to stop doing the task.

3. *Skill derivation.* With a task analysis in hand, it is possible to answer the question, "What would anyone have to know or be able to do before being ready to practice this entire task?" For example, before being ready to practice the task of interviewing a job applicant, anyone would have to be able to (a) interact tactfully, (b) speak

the applicant's language, and (c) complete an interview form. To complete the interview form may in turn require that the interviewer be able to (d) write legibly and/or (e) make computer entries.

In this way all of these skills that anyone would need to have are systematically derived from what competent interviewers actually do.

4. ***Objectives drafting.*** Now that the required skills have been derived from the task analyses, the next step is to draft objectives describing the limits—the "amount"— of skill that anyone would need to perform the various tasks. The objective describes the performance desired, the conditions under which the performance should occur, and the level of skill required.

The objectives describing the skills needed for performance of all of the job-related tasks provide the basis for development of a curriculum, a course, or coaching sessions.

The beauty of this procedure is that instructors who have derived objectives in this manner are able to prove that what they are teaching is relevant to the fulfillment of an important need.

5. ***Skill-hierarchy drafting.*** The next step is to draw a skill hierarchy that shows the prerequisite relationships between the objectives. A hierarchy looks a good deal like an organization chart and shows which skill needs to be mastered before another can be profitably practiced. For example, one needs to learn to speak a language before learning how to interact tactfully; one needs to be able to write before practicing writing reports or filling in forms. (See example on page 38.)

6. **Curriculum derivation.** To this point, the focus has been on what anyone would have to be able to do to perform competently in the target area (job, assignment, hobby, etc.). With objectives and hierarchy in hand, it is now possible to derive an efficient curriculum for each student or trainee by comparing the objective with what a given student can already do. If a given student can already do what one or more objectives require, these objectives are deleted from that student's curriculum.

Trainers expecting to work in business and industry must at the very least be able to perform the systematic objectives—deriving steps just described.

Now that we've taken a brief look at where objectives come from, it's time to consider the anatomy of an objective, so that you will be able to recognize a useful one when you see one and to draft your own.

4
The Qualities of Useful Objectives

Experience during recent decades has shown that instructional objectives are extremely important tools in the design, implementation, and evaluation of instruction. They are useful in pointing to the content and procedures that will allow instruction to be relevant and successful. They are useful in helping to manage the instructional process itself, and to point to the means for assessing instructional success.

Objectives in the hands of the students prevent the students from having to guess at how they might best organize their time and effort.

But what are the qualities of a useful objective? What characteristics would make one objective more useful than another?

Simply put, a usefully stated objective is one that succeeds in communicating an intended instructional result to the reader. It is useful to the extent that it conveys to others a picture of what a successful learner will be able to do; and to the extent that the picture it conveys is *identical to the picture the objective writer had in mind.*

Now, any number of combinations of words and pictures and symbols might be used to express an intended outcome.

What you are searching for is that group of words or symbols that will communicate your intent exactly as YOU understand it. For example, if you provide other instructors with an objective and they then teach some students to perform in a manner that *you agree* is consistent with what you had in mind, then you have communicated your objective in a meaningful manner. If, on the other hand, you "had something more in mind" or they didn't "grasp the essence" of your intent, then your statement failed to communicate adequately, regardless of how that statement was worded.

A meaningfully stated objective, then, is one that succeeds in communicating your intent; the best statement is the one that excludes the greatest number of possible meanings *other than* your intent.

Unfortunately, there are many slippery words that are open to a wide range of interpretation. (If you have tried to write more than a few sentences that say what you mean, you know how exasperating those little devils can be.) It isn't that such words aren't useful in everyday conversation. After all, you wouldn't want to be skewered with a "What do you mean by that?!" every time you said something like "It's a nice day," or "I really appreciate you," or "I'm fine." But if you use *only* such broad terms (or "fuzzies") when trying to communicate a specific *instructional* intent, you leave yourself open to *mis*interpretation.

Consider the following phrases in this light:

WORDS OPEN TO MANY INTERPRETATIONS	WORDS OPEN TO FEWER INTERPRETATIONS
to know	to write
to understand	to recite
to *really* understand	to identify
to appreciate	to sort
to *fully* appreciate	to solve
to grasp the significance of	to construct
to enjoy	to build
to believe	to compare
to have faith in	to contrast
to internalize	to smile

What do you mean when you say you want learners to know something? Do you mean you want them to recite or to solve or to construct? Just to tell them you want them to "know" tells them little—because the word can mean many different things. Until you say what you mean by "knowing" in terms of what students ought to be able to DO, you have said very little at all. Thus, an objective that communicates best will be one that describes the student's intended performance clearly enough to preclude misinterpretation.

How can you create this type of objective? What characteristics might help an objective to communicate and be useful? Several schemes might be used in stating objectives, but the format described on the following pages is known to work, and it is the one I have found easiest to use.

Three Characteristics to Include

The format includes three characteristics that help an objective to communicate an intent. These characteristics answer three questions:

- What should the learner be able to do?
- Under what conditions do you want the learner to be able to do it?
- How well must it be done?

1. **Performance.** An objective always states what a learner is expected to be able to do and/or produce to be considered competent.

   Example: Be able to ride a unicycle.

   (The performance stated is *ride*.)

   Example: Be able to write a letter.

   (The performance is *writing*; the product of the performance is a letter.)

2. **Conditions.** An objective describes the important conditions (if any) under which the performance is to occur.

   Example: Given a product and prospective customer, be able to describe the key features of the product.

   (The performance is to occur in the presence of a *product* and a *customer;* these are the conditions that will influence the nature of the performance, and so they are stated in the objective.)

3. **Criterion.** An objective describes the criteria of acceptable performance; that is, it says how well someone would have to perform to be considered competent.

> *Example:* Given a computer with word-processing software, be able to write a letter. Criteria: All words are spelled correctly, there are no grammatical or punctuation errors, and the addressee is not demeaned or insulted.
>
> (In this case the criteria of acceptable performance are labeled as such; often they are not.)

Sometimes there will be no special conditions to include, and sometimes it is impractical or useless to include a criterion (as when the criterion is obvious). But the more you say about your desired intent, the better you will communicate.

Characteristics That Should NOT Be Included in Objectives

It would be possible to add other features to objectives, such as instructional procedures, descriptions of the target audience, or format requirements.

Instructional procedure. For example, it would be possible to include a description of the procedure by which the objective will be accomplished, as in:

"Given six lectures on the subject of _____ . . ."

This feature would not serve a useful purpose, and it could be extremely limiting. What about an instructor who could accomplish the objective with only two lectures? Or with no lectures at all? Or could succeed by some other means? And what about the students who need no instruction at all? The objective should mention only outcomes, so that those charged with accomplishing those outcomes will be free to use their best wisdom and experience in doing so.

Imagine what would happen if industrial blueprints included information about how the products described should be manufactured. Aside from cluttering the blueprints and making them difficult or impossible to read, it would hamper those who had better ways to proceed than those described in the blueprint.

Target audience. Some people also describe the target audience for which the objective is intended, as in:

"First-line supervisors will be able to interview applicants . . ."

Such a feature would also get in the way. While it may be true that first-line supervisors need to be able to interview applicants, that might also be true for other groups. Should you have a different objective for each group, even though each of those objectives would say exactly the same thing?

In attempting to answer that question, I remember a school system whose teachers were required to write classroom objectives, course objectives, school objectives, district objectives, and county objectives. All those objectives described exactly the same performance, but the teachers went nuts trying to make them look different. In short, the answer is no.

Format. It would also be possible to insist that all objectives conform to a specific form or format. For example, one could expect all objectives to be written in a single sentence, or to begin with the conditions, or to not exceed a certain number of words. This again would be lunacy, as it would be another way to defeat the purpose of the objective, which is to describe a desired outcome.

I once visited a school in which teachers were expected to write their objectives on a form printed by the principal. His form had a line printed every two inches down the page, the implication being that every objective was no more than seven inches long and two inches high. Would you be surprised to learn that the teachers were hostile to the idea? But you are not looking for objectives that are a particular size and shape. You are looking for objectives that are *clear,* that say what you want to say about your instructional intents as concisely as possible. And that is all. So, anybody who says that an objective must be no more than two inches high and seven inches wide or who says an objective must or must not contain certain words should be reminded that the function of an objective is to communicate. If it does, rejoice. If it doesn't, fix it! You don't work on an objective until it matches someone's idea of "good looks"; you work on it until it communicates one of your instructional intents, and you write as many objectives as you need to describe ALL instructional results you think are important to accomplish.

The following chapters are intended to help you to do just that.

5
Performance

A useful objective includes these characteristics:

1. **Performance.** It describes what the learner is expected to be able to DO.

2. **Conditions.** It describes the conditions under which the performance is expected to occur.

3. **Criterion.** It describes the level of competence that must be reached or surpassed.

In this chapter we will investigate the first of these characteristics, that of performance. Performances may be visible, like writing, repairing, or painting; or invisible, like adding, solving, or identifying.

Visible (Overt) Performance

To be useful, an objective must state what it is that learners must do to demonstrate their mastery of the objective. This is easy to do when the main intent (the primary object of the objective) is visible or audible. For example, if the objective calls for students to be able to dance, or to interview, or to draft a report, the objective will state those visible/audible performances:

Be able to dance . . .

Be able to interview . . .

Be able to produce a report . . .

Can you tell directly when someone is dancing? Of course. Interviewing? Yes. Producing a report? Yes again. These are directly observable performances. In each of these instances the objective clearly states what it is that students are expected to be able to do, and each intended performance is directly visible and/or audible; you can see or hear someone doing it.

If a statement does not include a visible performance, it isn't yet an objective.

Many statements, however, only pretend to describe a performance. For example, consider the following:

To develop a critical understanding of the importance of effective management.

Though this may be an important goal, the statement doesn't tell you what someone would be doing when demonstrating mastery of the "objective." What would be your guess? Writing an essay on the importance of management? Answering multiple-choice questions on the history of management? Preparing a production schedule?

The statement not only doesn't say, it doesn't even provide a clue. In such cases it is highly unlikely that two or more people could agree on what the statement means; it is open to far too many interpretations. As an "objective" it is useless because it doesn't clearly communicate an intent.

Worse, the words "To develop . . ." suggest that the statement is referring to the *process* by which someone might come to have an understanding of the importance of effective management. Since you already know that objectives are about intended outcomes, you can see yet another defect in the above statement.

Now try this statement:

Given all available engineering data regarding a proposed product, be able to write a product profile. The profile must describe and define all of the commercial characteristics of the product appropriate to its introduction to the market, including descriptions of at least three major product uses.

What's the performance stated in the objective? Draw a circle around the words that tell you what the student will be doing when demonstrating achievement of the objective.

Check your response on page 55.

Given all available engineering data regarding a proposed product, be able to (write a product profile) The profile must describe and define all of the commercial characteristics of the product appropriate to its introduction to the market, including descriptions of at least three major product uses.

The student will be writing a product profile. Can you tell when someone is doing that? Yes. Therefore the statement includes a visible performance and so meets the first requirement of an objective.

The way to write an objective that meets the first requirement, then, is to draft a statement describing one of your intended instructional outcomes and then modify it until it answers the question:

What will the learner be DOING when demonstrating achievement of the objective?

Let's apply this test to some examples.

Which of the following statements is stated in performance terms? Turn to the page shown beside the answer you select.

Be able to write a news article. **Page 57.**

Be able to develop an appreciation of music. **Page 59.**

You said "Be able to write a news article" is written in performance terms. You've got it!

You remembered to apply the key question. What must people DO to demonstrate mastery of the objective? Why, they must write a news article. You can tell directly when they are doing that, so writing qualifies as a visible performance. You don't know whether the writing must be done by hand or on a keyboard, such as the one I am flogging at this very moment, but you do know that the main intent of the objective is writing. (NOTE: If the instrument of writing is important, that will be described as one of the conditions under which the performance is to occur.) For now, be content with performance.

Try another one. Turn to the page shown beside the statement that contains a performance.

Be able to understand mathematics.   *Page 65.*

Be able to sew a seam.   *Page 67.*

You said "Be able to develop an appreciation of music" was stated in performance terms. Gadzooks!

Maybe you thought so because the importance of the goal overshadowed the murkiness with which the goal was stated.

Ask the magic question: "What would someone be doing when demonstrating mastery of this goal?" Writing an essay on the meaning of opera? Sighing in ecstasy when listening to Bach? Answering multiple-choice questions on the history of music? Buying records? Stomping feet? The statement doesn't say. It doesn't give us a clue.

Let's consider performance a little more closely.

A performance is described by a *doing* word. If the word describes something you might be able to DO, then it describes a performance. If it only describes something you can BE, then it is not a *doing* word.

Here are some examples of *doing* words (performances):

> running
>
> solving
>
> writing

Here are some examples of *being* words (abstractions):

> happy
>
> understanding
>
> appreciating
>
> knowing

Turn to page 61.

You can see someone *running, solving,* or *writing.* Therefore those words qualify as performances.

But *appreciating* and *understanding* describe abstract states of being. That is, they describe states of being whose existence can only be *inferred* from performances. You can find out whether people understand something only by watching them act or by listening to them. You can tell whether they have a certain attitude only by watching them say or do something from which the existence of the attitude may be inferred.

See if you can tell the difference between performances (*doing* words) and abstractions (*being* words). **Circle the words below that describe performances:**

stating

writing

valuing

drawing

listing

appreciating

internalizing

smiling

When you have finished, turn to page 63.

Check your responses with mine. The performances are circled.

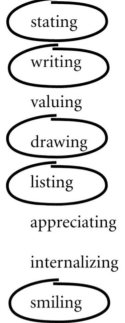

(stating)

(writing)

valuing

(drawing)

(listing)

appreciating

internalizing

(smiling)

The circled words describe things that people might do. The words not circled describe internal states of being. Valuing, for example, is not something that someone does; rather, it is something that is felt.

Now let's look at some statements and practice recognizing which ones include *performances*. Read the statements below, and turn to the page referred to beside the statement containing a *performance*.

Be able to understand mathematics.   **Page 65.**

Be able to sew a seam.   **Page 67.**

You said "Be able to understand mathematics" included a performance. Not for a minute.

What would people be *doing* when demonstrating their understanding? Defining mathematics? Writing an essay on Einstein? Solving problems? Correcting problems? Devising problems? The statement doesn't say anything about what someone might be expected to be able to do.

While *understanding* is a fine word for everyday conversation, it is open to far too many interpretations to be useful in an objective.

Try not to be trapped by the fact that the above statement begins with "be able to," as those words can be followed by sheer nonsense. Consider these slippery things:

Be able to develop an increased appreciation and sensitivity.

Be able to internalize a growing awareness.

What would someone be doing when internalizing a growing awareness? What would anyone be doing when developing an appreciation and sensitivity? I dunno. The statement doesn't say.

What we are looking for is the word or words that describe an intended action, whether that action be directly observable (running, writing, editing) or invisible (solving, recognizing, recalling).

Try another one. Turn to the page referred to beside the statement that contains a *performance:*

Be able to apply scientific knowledge. **Page 69.**

Be able to stain slides. **Page 71.**

You said "Be able to sew a seam" describes performance.

Yes. What are people doing when demonstrating their achievement of this objective? They are sewing something—that's what they are doing. We don't know whether there are any special conditions under which the seam sewing must occur, and we don't know how well someone would have to sew to be considered acceptable, but we do know that they have to sew seams (or so it seems). Thus, this statement meets the first requirement of an objective—it includes a performance.

Try another.

Turn to the page referred to beside the statement below that includes a performance:

Be able to apply scientific knowledge. **Page 69.**

Be able to stain slides. **Page 71.**

Well, I suppose I can understand how you might say that "apply scientific knowledge" states a performance. After all, the word *apply* sometimes DOES describe a performance. If the objective were about applying paint or applying makeup to a face, I would agree that I could tell when someone was doing the applying. But "applying scientific knowledge" is rather like "applying oneself with a proper attitude." You don't have the faintest idea of what the student would be doing. Singing a song? Taking out an appendix? Mixing a solution? Constructing a still? The statement doesn't give us any clue.

A statement ought not be called an objective unless, at the very least, it tells us what someone would have to do to demonstrate achievement of the objective. So, when you are looking for the performance, ask the question "What is the *doing* word?"

Turn to page 65 and reread.

You said "Be able to stain slides" includes a performance. Of course!

You can tell whether the stainer is staining the stainee. Therefore you can tell whether someone is doing what the objective says it is important to be able to do.

One final example. Which of the following statements includes a performance?

Develop a knowledge of food-service equipment.   Page 73.

Be able to add a column of numbers.   Page 75.

Come on!

How can I help you to internalize your growing awareness of infinite feeling states and consciousness levels if you keep slipping off to pages like these, "just to find out what is printed on them"?

As long as you're here, though, we might as well share a word or two about the topic at hand. *Develop* is one of those words which by itself doesn't tell you if it is describing a performance. All sorts of things might be developed—theses, neighborhoods, or triceps. But none of these is a performance; none describes anything anyone does. *Develop* is one of those words that depends on the words that follow it for its meaning, like "apply" and "demonstrate." Worse, it usually describes instructional *process,* and we want an objective to describe *outcome.*

There are other such sneakies. *Acquiring an attitude* is not at all the same as *acquiring a wallet.* The latter is a performance; the former is not.

Enough of diversion. Let's get back to work.

Read page 75.

You said "Be able to add a column of numbers" includes a performance. Yes.

What would someone be doing when demonstrating mastery of the objective? Adding a column of numbers. So the statement meets the first requirement of an objective.

Covert (Invisible) Performance

"Wait a minute," I hear you screaming, "something's fishy here. Someone could add while standing perfectly still! Or ogle, even. How can you call those performances when nobody can see them?"

Good point. As you've noted, some performances are not visible to the naked eye, such as solving, discriminating, and identifying. In these cases, statements that say:

Be able to solve . . .

Be able to discriminate . . .

Be able to identify . . .

are inadequate because they don't describe a visible performance. Though these and other invisible (covert) performances are often important, statements that describe only the covert performance are not yet objectives. Why? Because they don't tell us what someone must DO to demonstrate mastery of the objective.

Why not solve this problem simply by demanding that objectives describe only visible performance? Because a lot of the important performances we intend to nurture are covert (invisible), and to ignore them would prevent us from talking about a large part of our intended outcomes. As we are often interested in having students learn to solve problems, recognize specific characteristics, recall procedures, etc., the exclusion of this important part of our instruction would legitimately cause too many people to have a cow.

What to do? Simple, really. Whenever the main intent of your objective is covert, just add an indicator behavior to reveal how the covert performance can be directly detected. (Huh? Whut's an indicator?) An indicator behavior is one that will tell us directly whether a covert performance is happening to our satisfaction. An indicator is simple, direct, and always something that every trainee already knows how to do.

For example, if the objective is about an ability to discriminate counterfeit money, you would think it through as follows.

Hmm. The main intent of this objective is to be able to discriminate counterfeit money. But because I can't see anyone discriminating, I'll need to think of a way to find out whether the discriminating is happening. I know. I'll have them sort a pile of money into two piles. If they can do that correctly, I'll have a direct indication of their ability to discriminate. So all I have to do is to add the word "sort" to the objective, like this:

Be able to discriminate (sort) counterfeit money.

So we can write about covert performances in objectives as long as there is a direct way of finding out whether the performance is in good shape. "Direct way" means that there is a single act or behavior that will indicate the presence of the covert skill. The rule is this:

Whenever the performance stated in an objective is covert, add an indicator behavior.

That way, everyone will know what you mean when you use slippery words such as "identify." Just make sure the indicator you add is the simplest and most direct behavior you can think of, and make sure that it's something every trainee already knows how to do. Common examples are circle, underline, point to, write, say.

Occasionally I hear from someone who is disturbed about the use of the words "be able to" in an objective.

"I don't want them to be *able* to do things," goes the complaint, "I want them to DO them. Therefore, I think it's inappropriate to use those words in an objective."

Hmm. I can understand the source of the concern. But the purpose of an objective is to describe a capability you want them to carry around with them so that they can use it when they need or want to.

So I use "be able to" to describe the desired capabilities that should be available on demand.

When I want the capability actually demonstrated, I do so with a test. A test is a set of commands. "Answer these questions," "Interview this customer," and "Here's a symptom; locate the trouble," are examples of test items that ask for performance. If my objectives are couched in "demand language" rather than "capability language," they might confuse their users.

But if "be able to" pushes you into a psychic trauma, don't use it. Use whatever words will best communicate with your student populations.

Below are a few expressions, some of which describe covert performance and some of which describe overt performance. Here's what to do:

1. Place a check mark beside those expressions that describe performances that you can see or hear directly (overt).

2. Then, for those expressions describing covert performances, write the simplest, most direct indicator behavior you can think of that would tell you whether the covert performance existed.

Drive a bulldozer.   _____

Identify transistors on
a wiring diagram.   _____

Recognize tactless
statements.   _____

Discriminate between
normal and abnormal
X-rays.   _____

Paint a trombone.   _____

Dissect a politician.   _____

When you are ready, turn to page 80.

1. Drive a bulldozer. _____✓_____

2. Identify transistors on a wiring diagram.

   Circle
   _____

3. Recognize tactless statements.

   Point to; underline
   _____

4. Discriminate between normal and abnormal X-rays.

   Sort
   _____

5. Paint a trombone. _____✓_____

6. Dissect a politician. _____✓_____

1. You can watch someone driving a bulldozer, so you don't need an indicator to tell you that the performance happened.
2. But "identify" is a slippery word, and you need an indicator to let people know what you mean.
3. The same is true for "recognize." How do you want me to let you know that I have recognized to your satisfaction?
4. "Discriminate" usually means "be able to tell one thing from another," and you need an indicator to discover whether the covert discriminating occurred.

5, 6. You can watch people painting trombones and dissecting politicians, so no indicator behaviors are needed.

You see the point. When you can observe the main intent of the objective directly, just state the performance. But when the main intent is covert, add an indicator. The simplest way to do it is to write the indicator right after the performance, in parentheses, like this: "Be able to identify (sort) . . ."

Always State the Main Intent

Sometimes you will stumble over some objectives that state perfectly good indicators whose main intents are missing. For example:

> *Given completed Form 31s, be able to circle erroneous entries.*

What's the performance stated in the objective? Circling. But is circling what the objective is about? Hardly. The objective is about being able to *discriminate* (tell the difference between) correct and incorrect entries. So the objective should state that main intent:

> *Given completed Form 31s, be able to recognize erroneous entries.*

Because "recognize" describes a covert performance, it is useful to add an indicator behavior by which the presence of the covert performance may be detected. The simplest way is to state the main intent and then to follow it with the indicator in parentheses. Like so:

> *Given completed Form 31s, be able to recognize (circle) erroneous entries.*

Here's another example:

> *Given the brand names of products currently available to the cosmetologist, be able to underline those considered safe to use as shampoo.*

What's the performance stated in the objective? Underline. That's what it says. But do you suppose the writer of the objective is burning to have his/her students go through life underlining brand names? Doesn't seem likely, does it? Though the objective *says* underline, it's pretty clear that the objective writer has something more important in mind. In this example, it's easy to guess that the intent is for students to be able to discriminate—tell the difference—between safe and unsafe shampoos (or real poos, for that matter).

(Objectives like these—those that fail to state a main intent—are likely to be branded as trivial.)

Simply put, objectives aren't about indicators; they're about main intents. It's the main intent that students are supposed to learn. If they have to *learn* an indicator behavior, that behavior has absolutely no business being used as an indicator.

Summary

1. *An instructional objective describes an intended outcome of instruction, rather than the procedures for accomplishing those outcomes.*

2. *An objective always states a performance that describes what the learner will be DOING when demonstrating mastery of the objective.*

3. *When the main intent of an objective is covert, an indicator behavior—through which the main intent can be detected—is added.*

4. *Indicator behaviors are always the simplest, most direct behaviors possible, and they are always something that every trainee already knows how to do well.*

6
Conditions

By the time you have written an objective that says what you will expect your learners to do, you will have written a far less ambiguous objective than many which are in use today. Rather than expecting your students to guess what you have in mind when using such ambiguous words as *understand, know,* or *appreciate,* you will have at least revealed what you want them to accomplish. Regardless of how skimpy the statement may be, it will exhibit the most important characteristic of all—*it will be written down.* If it isn't written down, it isn't anything. If it is written down, it can be improved. And if it states a performance, it can be called an objective. Therefore, by the time your statement identifies a desired performance, you are more than halfway toward developing a useful objective.

But simply specifying the performance may not be enough to prevent serious misunderstanding of your intent. For example, suppose you are the master of ceremonies at the annual awards' night of the Whyners Club. As part of the program, you call me up from the audience and bet me a carload of broccoli that I can't lift the 500-pound barbells sitting on the stage.

I agree to the bet and then quickly get two burly types from the audience to help me, and we lift the barbells with ease.

"Where's my broccoli?" I ask.

"Wait a minnit," you reply. "You were supposed to lift those barbells by yourself."

"Oh? You didn't say that there were any *conditions* attached to this performance," I reply. "Why didn't you say so?"

"You should have *known* that I meant for you to do it by yourself."

"Sorry. My crystal ball hasn't come back from the cleaners. You'll just have to *keep* your broccoli," I say, snickering all the way back to my seat.

You can see how risky it can be to assume that others know what you are thinking. (If they *did* know what you were thinking, you'd have a lot more to worry about than the broccoli police.) You've had any number of experiences such as these during your school career: instances in which you were taught one thing and tested on another, for example, because the objectives weren't clear (if there were objectives at all).

To avoid surprises when working with objectives, we state the main intent of the objective *and* describe the main conditions under which the performance is to occur. An objective that says, "Be able to hammer a nail . . . " is different from one that says, "Given a brick, be able to hammer a nail . . . " If it just says, "Be able to hammer a nail . . . " you might assume that it means hammering with a hammer. That might be the logical assumption in the absence of any other information. But think how dismayed you would be if you practiced hammering with your hammer; but when it came time to demonstrate your skill, you were asked to hammer with a brick—or a stone—or a stapler. You would no doubt feel betrayed, tricked, and deceived—and you'd be right.

At the same time, you can imagine the writer of the objective looking up in total surprise, saying, "How could you *not* know I meant for you to hammer with a brick? You know perfectly well there are no hammers where you're going to be working." An objective such as "Be able to run the hundred-yard dash" may be stated in enough detail to prevent serious misunderstanding, provided the runners are not tricked by unexpected conditions such as having to run barefoot up a slippery slope—as the instructor shouts, "Hey, now. *Anybody* can run on level ground. That's no challenge."

Miscommunications such as these can be avoided by adding relevant conditions to your objective. How? Simply by describing the conditions that have a significant impact on the performance. By telling people what they will have, and not have, to work with when performing, and by telling them of special circumstances in which the performance must occur. In other words, by describing the givens and/or limitations within which the performance is expected to occur. Here are some examples:

Given a standard set of tools and the TS manual . . .

Using your service revolver . . .

Given a matrix of inter-correlations . . .

In the presence of an irate customer . . .

Without the aid of references . . .

With only a screwdriver . . .

On an obese patient, be able to . . .

On a fully functioning wrist computer . . .

How Much Detail?

How detailed should you be in your description? Detailed enough to describe each of the conditions that would be needed to allow the performance to happen; detailed enough to describe the conditions that would make a significant difference to the nature of the performance.

Here are some questions you can ask yourself to guide you in identifying key conditions.

1. What will the learner be expected to use when performing (e.g., tools, forms, etc.)?

2. What will the learner not be allowed to use while performing (e.g., checklists or other aids)?

3. What will be the real-world conditions under which the performance will be expected to occur (e.g., on top of a flagpole, under water, in front of a large audience, in a cockpit, etc.)?

Here is an example. Look at the objective below, and then turn to the page referred to under the part of the sentence that describes the conditions.

Given a list of factors leading to significant historical events,

Page 95.

be able to identify (underline) at least five factors

Page 89.

contributing to the Crash of 1929.

You said the phrase "be able to identify (underline)" describes conditions.

No, you selected the performance. Perhaps you're still thinking about the first important characteristic of an objective, the performance. If so, I'm glad you remembered it, but now we're attempting to identify (underline) the conditions under which the performance will be expected to occur.

Maybe it will help if you ask the question, "With what, or to what, will the learner be doing whatever it is he or she will be doing?"

Here's another example. Turn to the page number shown under the conditions.

Given a list of chemical elements,
Page 91.

be able to recall (write) the valences of each.
Page 93.

You've got it. "Given a list of chemical elements" is a condition that announces what will be provided during the expected performance, that of recalling valences.

Now identify (there's that sneaky word again) the conditions stated in the following objective. Turn to the page number shown under what you select as the conditions.

While blindfolded, and presented with wine samples, be able

Page 99.

to recognize (say) which samples were aged in oak casks.

Page 97.

No, you selected the performance, "be able to recall (write)," rather than the conditions, "Given a list of chemical elements."

Let me explain it this way. Suppose I said that you need to be able to recall the symbols and valences of chemical elements. With only that much information as a guide, you might go off to memorize all the symbols and their valences, only to discover that when it came time to perform, you would be provided with a list of the elements and asked to write their valences.

You might feel a little betrayed or deceived, because you spent all that time memorizing the symbols when, in fact, you would be provided with a list of them.

This can be an important point, because while doing your job you may often be provided with job aids in the form of checklists, procedures, lists of key steps, etc. These are intended to prevent you from having to memorize mountains of information. If you didn't know that these aids would be provided to help your performance, you might break your brain memorizing information that would, in fact, be provided to you.

Try this one: Turn to the page number shown under the conditions.

While blindfolded, and presented with wine samples, be able

Page 99.

to recognize (say) which samples were aged in oak casks.

Page 97.

You chose "Given a list of factors leading to significant historical events" as the words describing the conditions or situation under which the selecting behavior was to occur.

Correct. These words tell you that students will not be expected to choose factors from a library of books or from an essay on history or from their memories. The statement tells them that a list will be provided and that they will be expected to recognize rather than to recall.

Here is another example. Turn to the page number shown under the stated conditions.

Given a list of chemical elements,

Page 91.

be able to recall (write) the valences of each.

Page 93.

No, you chose the performance (recognize wine sample) rather than the conditions.

Maybe it would help to think of it like this. Imagine the performer standing in an empty field. With what would you have to provide this person before he or she would be able to do what the objective asks? Paper and pencil? A device or object? Another person?

The easy way to approach this task is like this:

1. First, circle the performance stated in the objective.

2. Then, look for conditions that would make a difference in how the performance is shaped.

Follow those two steps on this example. Circle the performance, and then underline the conditions.

Given a bag full of folded newspapers and a neighborhood street,

be able to throw a paper onto the roof of each house.

Now turn to page 101.

Got it! You correctly selected the conditions that were stated, "While blindfolded, and presented with wine samples."

Whenever you're not sure which is which, start by circling the performance (the DOING) words, and only then look for the conditions that might affect the performance. Of course, if no performance is stated, you'd be wasting your time to go any further. If it doesn't state a performance, it isn't an objective at all.

Try this example. Circle the performance, and then underline the conditions.

Without references, be able to recall (write) at least seven patient characteristics to which the therapist should respond and at least five characteristics to which the therapist should withhold response.

Turn to page 105.

Given a bag full of folded newspapers and a neighborhood street,

be able to throw a paper onto the roof of each house.

As you can see, circling the performance makes it a lot easier to decode the objective. If there is no performance stated, you're not dealing with an objective, so you can stop right there (or run screaming to the objective writer for more information).

Once the performance has been circled, it is easier to answer the question, "What are the conditions under which the performance will occur?"

Here's another example. Circle the performance, and then underline the conditions.

Given a malfunctioning DC motor of ten horsepower or less, a kit

of tools, and references, be able to repair the motor.

Turn to page 103.

An objective need not consist of only a single sentence. On the contrary, quite a few sentences might be required to communicate your intent clearly. This is often true, for example, when you are describing objectives requiring creative activity on the part of the learner. Here is one such example:

> *Be able to write a musical composition with a single tonal base within four hours. The composition must be at least sixteen bars long and must contain at least twenty-four notes. You must apply at least three rules of good composition in the development of your score.*

Here is another example, this one from a workshop designed to prepare participants to design performance-based instruction.

> **Given:** *A list of ideal course characteristics, learning-environment description, skill hierarchies, objectives, skill checks, and the course procedures for this course.*
>
> **Performance:** *Be able to draft a list of procedures by which your course will operate.*
>
> **Criteria:** *a. The procedures are as consistent with ideal characteristics as constraints will allow.*
> *b. The list at the very least includes procedures describing how students are to proceed in regard to (1) course attendance and working hours, (2) module completion, (3) location and use of resources, (4) skill checks, and (5) module sign-off.*
> *c. The procedures are written to be understood by your target population.*

Given a malfunctioning DC motor of ten horsepower or less, a kit

of tools, and references, be able to(repair)the motor.

If your work matches the above, you're doing fine. If it doesn't, here's another question to ask when hunting for conditions:

What would it take to make this performance possible?

Here's one last example before we move to the third characteristic of a useful objective. Circle the performance, and then underline the conditions.

Without references, be able to recall (write) at least seven patient

characteristics to which the therapist should respond and at least

five characteristics to which the therapist should withhold

response.

Turn to page 105.

Without references, be able to recall (write) at least seven patient characteristics to which the therapist should respond and at least five characteristics to which the therapist should withhold response.

About the only special condition mentioned here is "without references." Everything else tells you what the students are to do and how well they have to be able to do it.

QUESTION: If the objective doesn't *say* the students can use references, can't you presume that they will have to work without them? Can't you *assume* that "no references" is intended? Isn't it a fair inference? Since I can't tell what is in the mind of the objective writer, I can't tell whether it is a fair inference or not. But when you're writing an objective, why take a chance on having your objective misinterpreted when you don't have to? Why not simply add a few words to say what you mean? Then the reader will know for sure, rather than for maybe.

Turn to page 106.

How Many Conditions?

How finely should conditions be described? Should every objective state conditions?

The answers to these questions are: Add enough description to an objective to make it clear to everyone concerned just what you expect from the learner. If what you expect is made clear just by stating the desired performance and the degree of excellence you desire (the criterion), then don't add conditions arbitrarily. How can you tell whether the conditions are defined clearly enough? Give your draft objective to a couple of students, and ask them what they think they would have to do to demonstrate their mastery of the objective. If their description matches what you have in mind, then you have done well. If it doesn't, then a little patching here or there is in order. But remember the ironclad rule of objective writing:

If there is disagreement about the meaning, don't argue about it—fix it!

For now, you have had enough practice with identifying conditions to have the basic idea. There will be more practice later on to sharpen up your skill, so let's move on to the final characteristic of a useful objective, the criterion of acceptable performance.

Summary

1. *An instructional objective describes an intended outcome of instruction, rather than the procedures for accomplishing those outcomes.*

2. *An objective always states a performance describing what the learner will be DOING when demonstrating mastery of the objective.*

3. *When the main intent of an objective is covert, an indicator behavior—through which the main intent can be detected— is added.*

4. *Indicator behaviors are always the simplest, most direct behaviors possible, and they are always something that every trainee already knows how to do well.*

5. *To prepare an objective:*

    a. *Write a statement that describes the main intent or performance expected of the student.*

    b. *If the performance happens to be covert, add an indicator behavior through which the main intent can be detected.*

    c. *Describe relevant or important conditions under which the performance is expected to occur. Add as much description as is needed to communicate the intent to others.*

7
Criterion

Once you have described what you want students to be able to do (the performance) and the circumstances in which you want them to do it (the conditions), you will have given them far more information about your intents than they are accustomed to receiving. With performance and conditions made clear, it will no longer be necessary for them to wonder how best to focus their efforts.

There is something else you can do, though, to increase the communicating power of your objective: Add a criterion of acceptable performance. This will tell students how well they will have to perform to be considered competent. By adding information about the yardstick by which accomplishment of the objective will be measured, you will enormously strengthen the usefulness of your objectives. You will have gained several advantages.

1. You will have a standard against which to test the success of the instruction.

2. Students will know how to tell when they have met or exceeded the performance expectations.

3. You will have the basis for proving that your students can, in fact, do what you set out to teach them.

Those are powerful benefits in the quest for improved performance.

What you must do, then, is complete your objectives by adding information that describes the criterion for success. Remember that if it isn't measurable, it isn't an objective. What we are now turning our attention to is the issue of just what should be measured.

Before you proceed, however, turn to the page that best describes your feeling at this moment.

Many of the things I teach are intangible and CANNOT be evaluated. *Page 113.*

Show me how to describe criteria of acceptable performance. *Page 115.*

Occasionally someone asks, "Why bother with objectives? If you have good test items, aren't objectives redundant?"

It is a question that deserves comment.

Perhaps I can clarify the relationship between objectives and test items by rephrasing the question this way: "If you have a ruler with which to measure the dimensions of a building, why do you need a blueprint?" Answer: So that anyone will know whether the completed building looks the way it was intended to look and so that similar buildings can be constructed if desired.

The same is true of objectives. If you had only test items, you wouldn't know what critical characteristics were important to develop, you wouldn't know how to determine whether the main intent had been achieved, and you wouldn't know how to tell whether students were competent enough to be considered acceptable.

Thus, the objective describes where you are going, while the test items are the means by which you find out whether you got there.

Well . . . all right . . . but if you are teaching things that cannot be evaluated, you are in the awkward position of being unable to demonstrate that you are teaching anything at all. Though it is sometimes appropriate for a course to be aimed at providing opportunities for students to explore or debate ideas (process), our concern here is with instruction whose purpose is to accomplish important learning results (outcomes).

The "My subject is intangible" approach is risky for at least two reasons. First, it lulls people into thinking they are saying something when they are not. For example, how would you know whether this "objective" was achieved?

After having studied a variety of forms of non-verbal communication, the student is able to demonstrate an ability to send and receive non-verbal messages.

To cast "objectives" in such vague language serves only to confuse students, as well as those charged with development of the instruction. It is the lazy approach to instruction.

Second, the "My subject is intangible" conviction simply isn't true. You already make decisions about whether or not students can or cannot perform to your satisfaction, and with a little effort you can describe the basis for that satisfaction. In other words, you can say what students would have to say or do for you to agree that they had accomplished the "intangible" result. If it is important that your students learn something of consequence, it is important to find out whether or not you have succeeded in teaching them. Hiding behind the "intangible" myth won't help.

Turn to page 115.

Perhaps you have had academic experiences similar to this one. During class periods of a seventh-grade algebra course, a teacher provided a good deal of skillful guidance in the solution of simple equations and made sure that all students had enough practice to give them confidence in their ability. When it came time for an examination, however, the test items consisted mainly of stated (word) problems, and the students performed rather poorly. The teacher's justification for this "sleight of test" was that the students didn't "really understand" algebra if they could not solve word problems.

Perhaps the teacher was right. But the skill of solving equations is considerably different from the skill of solving word problems; if he wanted his students to learn how to solve word problems, he should have taught them how to do so.

Don't expect a learner to be able to exhibit Skill B simply because you have given practice in Skill A.

All right, let's consider some of the ways to add criteria of acceptable performance to your objectives.

Note that we are not looking to specify a *minimum* or *barely tolerable* criterion. We are looking for ways to describe the *desired* or *appropriate* criterion. Sometimes that means a low performance level is OK, and sometimes it means that only perfect performance is OK. Sometimes it means that considerable error can be tolerated, and sometimes it means that no errors can be tolerated. For example, while it might be acceptable for a shipping clerk to tie an occasional knot that slips, surgeons are expected to tie knots that don't slip. Ever.

Speed

One of the common ways to describe a criterion of acceptable performance is to describe a *time limit* within which a given performance must occur. Such a time limit is often implied when you tell students how long an examination period will be. If the speed of performance is important, however, it is better to be explicit about it; then no one will have to guess at what you have in mind for them to do. When time is of the essence, it is only fair to communicate that criterion to the learner. For example, consider this:

Instructor:	You flunk!
Student:	But I ran the hundred-yard dash, like you said.
Instructor:	True. But you were too slow.
Student:	But you didn't say how fast we had to run.
Instructor:	Would I ask you to run if I didn't want you to run fast? You should have known that speed was important.

You might also write the objective on page 117 by using this format:

Conditions: *Dry, level track.*

Performance: *Run the hundred-yard dash.*

Criterion: *Within fourteen seconds.*

This format is especially useful for more complex objectives.

If speed is important, say so in the objective, and more people will perform as you intend.

If you do NOT intend to evaluate a performance on the basis of its speed, you need not and should not impose a time limit. The rule is to impose only those criteria that are important. If it is important that the running be done to a speed criterion, then the objective might better read:

Be able to run the hundred-yard dash on a dry, level track within fourteen seconds.

Then all the students would know what they should do, where they should do it, and how fast they should do it.

Let's try a little practice in recognizing criteria in an objective. Read the following objective and then turn to the page below the words that describe the criterion of acceptable performance (the words that tell how well the learner must be able to perform the task).

Given tools, references, and a malfunctioning centrifugal pump, be able to clear the malfunction within fifteen minutes.

Page 119. **Page 121.**

Turn to the page number that brackets the criterion.

You said that "be able to clear the malfunction" is a criterion of acceptable performance. No, I think you may still be thinking about performance rather than about quality of performance. Performance is critical, of course, but the words you chose tell what the learner is expected to do, not how well it is to be done.

When looking for criteria, look for the answer to the question, "How well does the learner need to perform to achieve the objective?"

When the criterion relates to speed, look for words that tell you how fast something needs to be done (e.g., within five seconds), words that tell you what has to be done before another event begins (e.g., before the red light comes on), or words that tell you how often something must be done per unit of time (e.g., must fire at least three rounds within two seconds).

Turn to page 117 and read the item again.

You said that "within fifteen minutes" is the criterion. You've got it.

For this objective, it doesn't matter whether the performer uses a wrench or a hammer to get the job done; what matters is that the malfunction is cleared within fifteen minutes. How will you find out whether someone has met this criterion? Simple. Provide the student with a malfunctioning pump, some tools, and references; ask him or her to fix it within fifteen minutes, and time the performance. If the pump is fixed within fifteen minutes, the criterion of acceptable performance will have been met.

How Many Pumps?

You may be thinking, "I wouldn't consider them competent if they repaired only one pump. I'd want to see them repair a range of malfunctions before I'd be willing to stamp them US Choice." Good point. It makes a lot of sense to expect people to perform under the range of conditions described in the objective before agreeing that they have achieved the objective. But though this is good practice, it relates more to how you test rather than to how you write the objective. If you're not careful, you can find yourself writing test items and calling them objectives. For example:

Given five malfunctioning pumps, be able to fix them . . .

smells like a test item. Why? Because the main intent is for people to be able to repair malfunctioning pumps. Not five pumps or two pumps, but however many malfunctioning pumps come along. To include, "Given five pumps . . ." in the objective will confuse the objective (what they need to be able to do) with the test situation (how you will find out whether they can do it).

Accuracy

Speed is only one way to determine a criterion of success. Sometimes the accuracy of a performance is more important than its speed, and sometimes both speed and accuracy are important.

Here's an example of an accuracy criterion:

Be able to state the time shown on the face of any clock to within one minute of accuracy.

Since the rapidity of the performance is unimportant, no speed criterion is shown.

Or your objective might include criteria like these:

. . . and solutions must be accurate to the nearest whole number.

. . . with materials weighed accurately to the nearest gram.

. . . correct to at least three significant figures.

. . . with no more than two incorrect entries for every ten pages of log.

. . . listening carefully enough that no more than one request for repeated information is needed for each customer contact.

. . . with all surfaces finished to a 64 smoothness tolerance.

Use whatever word or means that will communicate how well your students must perform before you will agree that they have achieved the objective.

Now answer this question. Which of the following includes an accuracy criterion? Turn to the page number shown beside your selection.

Given a yard of baloney and a sharp knife, be able to cut the baloney into slices no more than one centimeter thick.

Page 129.

Be able to visualize with 90 percent accuracy. *Page 127.*

You said that "Be able to visualize with 90 percent accuracy" included an accuracy criterion. I can see how you might think so. After all, the sentence actually includes the word "accuracy."

But just what is it that someone would be doing? Visualizing? Visualizing *what*? Angels on the head of a pin? Electrons in a cyclotron? How your amour might look in iron underwear? Don't be deceived by the fact that a percentage is stated. If the description of accuracy doesn't make any sense— that is, if it doesn't tell you clearly how well you must perform—it isn't a criterion. Here are some other silly non-objectives.

Be able to internalize a growing awareness with 90 percent accuracy.

Be able to dramatize an increasing sensitivity. Criterion: nine out of ten dramatizations must be correct.

Be able to compose a sonata with 90 percent accuracy.

As you can see, it's not a criterion just because it contains a number. The number has to make sense, which means it has to refer to a genuine performance and it has to describe a limit to that performance.

Return to page 125 and read the item again.

Let's split a hair.

As you work with objectives, you will notice that while the performances stated therein tell you what people are expected to be able to DO, the criteria often may describe the characteristics (or shapes) of the PRODUCTS of that doing. When, for example, objectives ask that someone be able to:

- write a report

- construct an amplifier

- repair a word processor

the criteria will describe the desired characteristics of the *products* of those performances. The criteria will say something about the characteristics of the *final* report, the *completed* amplifier, or the *repaired* word processor, rather than about *how* those products were produced (the shapes of the performances).

"So what?" I hear you muttering. So not a whole lot. It's just that, in these instances, you determine whether the performance is adequate by looking at the product of the performance rather than at the performance itself. And you make darn sure you don't allow people to be evaluated on the shape of their *performance* when it is the shape of the *product* that is important. Don't allow the sort of evaluation that says, "Oh, sure, her report is terrific in all respects, but she wrinkles her nose when she types, so we'll have to take ten points off."

It's "nice to know" the distinction between performance and its product, because sometimes your criteria will need to describe performance *or* product, and sometimes some of both. But your attention should be directed toward describing the criteria that matter, regardless of their labels.

Yes. The objective you selected has an accuracy criterion, and that's no baloney. The objective tells you that the baloney must be cut accurately enough so that no slice is thicker than one centimeter.

Given a yard of baloney and a sharp knife, be able to cut the baloney into slices no more than one centimeter thick.

It doesn't matter how long you take to do it or how many slices you ruin or drop on the floor. Performers will have achieved the objective if they meet the single accuracy criterion stated.

Quality

Many times the speed or accuracy of a performance is not critical. Instead, something about the quality of the performance must be present if the performance is to be considered acceptable. For example, in our Criterion-Referenced Instruction (CRI) Workshop, one module requires trainees to learn to answer questions on their feet about CRI, so that they'll be able to handle themselves well in a give-and-take discussion about the subject.

But what does that mean? How much give and how much take? Clearly a speed criterion is not appropriate, because in real life it doesn't matter how fast one speaks. The first criterion listed is an accuracy criterion, but the others refer more to the quality of the responses. Here's how we wrote this objective:

In an interview, and without references or notes, be able to respond correctly to questions relating to criterion-referenced instruction. Criteria:

  a. All information offered is factual.
  b. Information is pertinent to the questions.
  c. Questioners are treated courteously (they are not insulted or demeaned).
  d. Jargon is defined when it is first introduced.

You can see that it would be possible to clutter this objective with criteria referring to many other aspects of the performance, none of which would make a difference to the quality of the responses. The trick is to confine oneself to describing only those criteria that are important to the way the performance will be expected to occur after the instruction is ended.

Where Do Criteria Come From?

How will you know whether a criterion should require that a performance be completed in ten minutes or twenty minutes? Or that it should demand brushing your teeth with more than one pound of pressure rather than less than a pound of pressure? Or that the objective should call for ten customer calls per day rather than five? In other words, where do (or should) criteria come from? There are four general sources from which criteria may be dictated or derived.

Job Requirements

Those who derive objectives from real world needs will observe and interview competent and/or exemplary performers and describe what the performers do and how well they do it. They will then use this information as the basis for deriving objectives and the criteria that should be attached.

For example, if competent pie-throwers actually hit their targets at least eight times out of ten throws, an "80% hits" criterion might be added to the pie-throwing objective. Why not make it 100? Because any idiot can write an objective that says, "Be able to do this or that with 100% accuracy." That doesn't mean it's a better criterion, and it doesn't mean it's a realistic criterion. Remember, perfection costs money; the tighter the criteria, the costlier the training. It's like smoothness; the smoother you want the surface machined, the more it will cost. Any time you see an objective that calls for perfection (i.e., "100% accuracy"), attack it. Make the objective writer defend that as a realistic criterion.

Sometimes the criteria will be set at entry level. In these instances the criteria will be set to reflect what employers require in the way of entry-level skill (what it will take to get the job in the first place), rather than what the employee will be like after extensive experience and practice. When a manager says, "I can't hire tellers who can't count," it is wise to find out what "can't count" means and then set a criterion accordingly.

Improvement Requirements

Another source of criteria can be the requirements that must be met if performance improvement is expected to occur as a result of practice alone. What this means is that criteria are set to reflect the answer to the question:

"How much entry-level skill does someone need in order for practice alone *to lead to improvement?"*

For example, if someone leaves the training environment able to solder three joints per minute correctly and *without supervision,* that person has all the skill needed to improve with practice. If someone is willing to hire this person at that skill level, the employer will know that the skill will improve with practice (provided that the employer gives *opportunities* for practice before the skill deteriorates).

If, however, the criteria are set so low that improvement would require more than just practice (e.g., coaching), then the skill will either deteriorate or the performer will learn to do it wrong.

Academic Requirements

Derivation of appropriate objectives and criteria in the academic environment is easier. (It's technically easier, but it's often a nightmare politically—because of turf battles.)

Suppose, for example, that you are assigned to teach Algebra I and set out to derive objectives for that course. (No, no. Don't go to the textbook; use a more rational approach.) One source of objectives for your course would be the prerequisites of Algebra II. So you would go to whomever is teaching the advanced course to find out just what the entry-level expectations are for that course. If that instructor gives you a list of objectives, and tells you, "These are the things I expect students to be able to do when they enter my course," you will have a good idea of what your students should be able to do when they leave *your* course. Thus, the prerequisites for the next course(s) will tell you a lot about what objectives and criteria should be for the preceding course.

This isn't the only source from which your criteria may be derived. For example, if one of the consumers of your students will be the local community, you can take steps to answer the question, "What do these students need to be able to do, and how well, to function successfully in their community?" and set your criteria accordingly.

Personal Experience

Another guide to criteria (but not always the best) comes from personal wisdom and experience. People who are actually performing the skills described by the objectives in real-world settings are likely to have good insights into the performance quality needed to do the job well. Thus, if you are drafting objectives and are at the same time living the skills you're writing about, your judgments about appropriate criteria would be valuable. If, however, you don't actually do the things the objectives describe, then don't rely on your judgments; go to competent performers and derive the criteria from their performances.

Pointing to the Criterion

There are at least three ways to indicate a criterion without actually describing the criterion in the objective. All are ways of pointing to the criterion:

1. If an intended criterion has been made *explicit* in some document or other, the thing to do in the objective is to add words that tell where to find the criterion. For example:

   . . . according to the Standard Chart, 2023 edition.

   . . . Criterion: manufacturer's specifications, *Repair Manual, Corrugated Soap,* 2023 edition.

   . . . according to the criteria described on p. 33, *Manual* 27-10.

This procedure should be used, however, only when the criteria are clearly stated in the reference you are pointing to and only when that reference is readily available to the performers.

2. If the desired performance consists of a number of steps and if an evaluation checklist exists, you might point to that checklist as a description (or partial description) of the criteria. For example:

   . . . Criterion: All steps to be performed as well as, and in the sequence described by, the Cheeky Checklist of Proper Kissing.

   . . . with each action to compare in quality (sequence is not important) with the Performance Checklist of Turgid Terpsichore.

3. On rare occasions you might find it appropriate to point to competent performance shown on a piece of film, videotape, CD, etc., saying, in effect, "Do it like *that.*" This might be useful if the performance involves

complex movements difficult to describe, such as dance steps, diving, or underwater maneuvers. I hesitate to mention this method, however, for fear that someone will take it as a license to use *only* the dynamic media without also describing the key characteristics of the desired performance in the objective itself. Such a practice would be almost as uninformative as that other false criterion, "to the satisfaction of the instructor." Refer to film, videotape, or documents only if they help in making the desired criteria clear to all concerned.

Condition or Criterion?

Sometimes it is not easy to read an objective and tell whether a phrase describes a condition or a criterion. Sometimes the two rather blend together. For example:

Be able to do consecutively thirty push-ups, thirty sit-ups, and thirty pull-ups without the use of mechanical aids.

What is the criterion? The *number* of acts that must be performed? Yes, but some would call it a condition. Some would say that "without the use of mechanical aids" also is part of the criterion. Their argument would go this way: A criterion tells how good a performance must be, and in this case the performance must be good enough to be done without aids. Who is right?

Doesn't really matter, as long as the intent of the objective is clear. The problem here is caused by the wording. If the objective had been worded like this:

Without the use of mechanical aids, be able to do consecutively push-ups, sit-ups, and pull-ups. Criterion: thirty each push-ups, sit-ups, and pull-ups.

or like this:

Performance:	Do consecutive push-ups, sit-ups, and pull-ups.
Conditions:	Without the use of mechanical aids.
Criterion:	Thirty each.

there would be no question about which is a condition (something that influences the shape of the performance), and which is a criterion (something that tells how much performance is required). What is important is that an objective be refined until it communicates the intent of the writer. If it answers the following questions, I would consider it a useful objective, regardless of whether everyone agreed on the labels for the phrases:

- What is the main intent of the objective?

- What does the learner have to do to demonstrate achievement of the objective?

- What will the learner have to do it with or to? And what, if anything, will the learner have to do it without?

- How will we know when the performance is good enough to be considered acceptable?

If you cannot specify a criterion with as much clarity as you would like, or if you can't even *begin* to decide what the critical criteria are for an objective, use the "Hey, Gofer" ploy. That is, you first think to yourself, "Hey, Gofer. I want you to find out whether these people have, or have not, achieved this objective . . . and here's what I want you to look for." Then jot down the instructions that will tell Gofer how to decide whether the learners have or have not achieved the objective. This ploy is especially useful when your head is stuck in the "It's intangible" mode.

Summary

1. *An objective is a collection of words, symbols, and/or pictures describing one of your important intents.*

2. *An objective will communicate your intent to the degree you describe what the learner will be DOING when demonstrating achievement of the objective, the important conditions of the doing, and the criterion by which achievement will be judged.*

3. *To prepare a useful objective, continue to modify a draft until these questions are answered:*

    *   *What do I want students to be able to do?*

    *   *What are the important conditions or constraints under which I want them to perform?*

    *   *How well must students perform for me to be satisfied?*

4. *Write a separate statement for each important outcome or intent; write as many as you need to communicate your intents.*

5. *If you give your written objectives to your students, you may not have to do much else. Why? Because often students are already able to do what you are asking them to do and will be happy to demonstrate their ability, now that they know what is wanted of them.*

8
Pitfalls and Barnacles

Over recent decades, those of us involved in the systematic design and implementation of instruction have seen many ways in which objectives have been used—and misused. On the one hand, we've seen objectives used as a tool for tailoring instruction to the needs of the individual student and for delivering instruction in ways that minimize learning time. On the other hand, we've seen the most ludicrous statements parading as objectives, we've seen statements with confusing phrasing and useless words, and we've seen profound-sounding statements that couldn't be of any use whatsoever. In short, we've seen objectives used in highly productive ways, and we've seen them used in ways that impeded the progress of instructors and students alike. This chapter describes the most-frequently seen troublesome objectives.

False Performance

This point was made earlier, but its importance warrants some repetition. One of the most pervasive defects of statements that are mistakenly called objectives is that they have the appearance of objectives but contain no performances;

therefore, they are not objectives at all. Here are some examples:

- Have a thorough understanding of particle physics.
- Demonstrate a comprehension of the short-story form.
- Be able to relate to others in a demonstration of empathy.
- Be able to think critically and analytically.
- Be able to understand individual differences in patients.
- Know how to conduct a sales interview.
- Know how to appreciate the importance of corporate strategy.

Expressions such as these may describe some important goals in very broad terms. However, they are not objectives, because they do not state what someone would have to do to demonstrate mastery of the unstated main intent.

When statements without performances are thought of as objectives, they lead to a variety of confusions. People are likely to argue about which instructional procedure is suitable for accomplishing the vaguely stated intent and are frustrated when the statement offers no firm guidelines. They cannot agree on methods for assessing achievement of the intent and may complain that all objectives are useless. The instructor is at a loss in understanding why the *students* are at a loss in understanding what they are expected to be able to do. Little wonder, as broad statements provide few clues to action.

When interpreting or drafting an objective, you must first look for the performance. Draw a circle around it. If there isn't a performance to draw a circle around, it isn't an objective—yet. Fix it or forget it.

False Givens

Another common error (in the sense that it does not help in

communicating an instructional intent) is the inclusion of false givens. These are words or phrases that may follow the word *given* in an objective but that describe something *other* than specific conditions the learner must have or be denied when demonstrating achievement of the objective. Most typically, the words describe something about the instruction itself, such as the following:

Given three days of instruction on . . .

Given that the student has completed six laboratory experiments on . . .

Given that the student is in the category of gifted . . .

Given adequate practice in . . .

Here are other examples, actually labeled as conditions in the objective:

Conditions: Pre-course reading material that overviews the managerial leadership process.

Conditions: Discussion group.

Conditions: a) Competent instructors.
b) One's own knowledge of regional organization.

Because none of these items has anything to do with describing the conditions affecting the performance stated in the objective, they are ripe for the charge of "false givens."

As indicated earlier, an objective is useful to the degree that it communicates an intended outcome. If you allow it to describe instructional procedure, you will restrict all concerned in using their best wisdom and experience to help accomplish that outcome. Make sure that the conditions described in your objectives tell something about the situation in which you expect the student to demonstrate competence.

Teaching Procedures

Related to the false givens is the error of writing an objective to describe a teaching point, a practice exercise, or some other aspect of classroom activity. For example, consider this:

Be able to choose an art print or photo that illustrates a theme of your choice and explain how it illustrates that theme.

Why would you want a student to do such a thing? Certainly it isn't because a meaningful thing to do in the world is to go around explaining to people the theme that's illustrated by a photo you have chosen. Presumably, the reason for wanting students to engage in this activity is that it will help them learn to do something that *can* be considered a meaningful skill. For example:

Givens: *A theme.*
                   Collection of art prints and/or photos.

Performance: *Identify (point to) the prints/photos that illustrate the theme.*

Criterion: *At least 60% of your choices match the choices of a panel of art experts.*

The argument is not with the usefulness of having students practice selecting prints and explaining themes; the argument is with writing descriptions of such activities and calling them objectives. There are two practical reasons for this argument: 1) if you describe all instructional activities or teaching points and call them objectives, you will be up to your . . . er . . . a . . . well, you'll be drowning in verbiage (this is why some teachers complain that there are too many objectives); 2) the main function of an objective is to help course planners decide on instructional content and procedure. If the objective describes a teaching procedure, it will fail to perform its primary purpose, because it will be describing instructional practice rather than important instructional outcomes.

You can avoid this problem by asking yourself *why* you want students to be able to do what you've described in each objective you draft. If your answer is "Because *that* is one of the things they need to be able to do when they leave here," then the objective can probably stand. If, however, your answer is "So that they will then be able to _____," and you fill in the blank with something *other* than what the draft objective describes, then that draft objective may describe a teaching procedure. If so, it should be modified to describe the desired outcome, instead. Here is another example:

Be able to discuss in class the case histories handed out by the instructor.

Why did this instructor want students to be able to discuss written case histories in class? Her answer was something like this: "Because if they are going to be able to solve problems, they need to be able to tell the difference between statements of fact and statements of opinion. The discussion of case histories gives them practice in doing that." Ah so. Her response made it clear that her original objective described a teaching procedure rather than an intended outcome, a means rather than an end. She would find this objective more useful,

therefore, if she modified it to describe the reason for the practice activity of case discussions:

> *Given written descriptions of problem situations involving*
> *interactions, be able to identify (label) statements of fact and*
> *statements of opinion.*

Write your objectives about things you want your students
to be able to do when they leave you, and you will avoid
drowning in trivia.

Gibberish

A problem similar to that of the false performance is that
sometimes the so-called objectives either contain, or are com-
posed entirely of, phrases with little or no meaning. The following are examples of worthless expressions:

Manifest an increasing comprehensive understanding . . .

Demonstrate a thorough comprehension . . .

Relate and foster with multiple approaches . . .

Have a deep awareness and thorough humanizing grasp . . .

When such words are followed by a description of desired
performance, they are not disastrous; they just get in the way.
If they are not so followed, the danger is more substantial. The
danger is that people will be lulled into thinking something
meaningful has been said and then may question their own
sanity or intelligence because they fail to perceive the meaning
that isn't there. For example, "Demonstrate the ability to make
practical application of information in a creative way." What in
the world would someone be doing when demonstrating mastery of such a fogged intent? When you see an entire statement

like that, which consists of a meaningless combination of words and symbols, you can understand why some people complain that objectives are useless. Consider the following:

Embark on a lifelong search for truth, with the willingness and ability to pose questions, examine experience, and construct explanations and meanings.

Develop a thorough understanding of the corporate culture, to include policies on harassment, ethnic diversity, and equal access to individual counseling.

The student must be able to demonstrate an ability to develop self-confidence and self-respect.

Verbiage such as this may seem impressive, but it is of little use in communicating instructional intents. Nor can I offer an improved version of these statements, as I don't know what their writers were trying to convey. Fortunately, there is a simple solution.

The best way to degibberize an objective is to give it to a couple of students and ask them what they think it means. While their utterances may sometimes be a little hard on the ego, those utterances will usually show the way toward a cleaner, simpler statement of your intent.

And don't forget editors. A good editor can make miraculous moves toward simplicity and clarity by changing just a few words here and there, and I am continually amazed at how helpful they can be. (You have to watch them, though, for many are slaves to their style manuals and are sometimes willing to sacrifice meaning in their push for conformity.)

Instructor Performance

Another practice that interferes with the usefulness of an objective is that of describing what the instructor is expected to do rather than what the student is expected to be able to do.

The instructor will provide an atmosphere that will promote the development of self-esteem, confidence, and security.

The teacher will help the student recognize natural consequences of behavior.

The instructor will assist the student in the development of . . .

Demonstrate to students the proper procedures for completing Form 321.

Phrases such as these might properly describe an instructor objective or an administrative objective, but they say nothing about what results are to be expected insofar as student competence is concerned. Similarly, statements that begin:

Each student will . . .

Eighty percent of the students will . . .

have no meaning to a student, either. What can a student do about an "objective" that says "70 percent of the students must be able to demonstrate an ability to read"? Such statements may provide the basis for instructor objectives, but they are of no help to students.

An instructional objective describes student performance; it avoids saying anything about instructor performance. To do otherwise would unnecessarily restrict individual instructors from using their best wisdom and skills to accomplish the objective.

When reviewing your draft objective, ask whether it is referring to student performance. If so, rejoice; if not, revise.

False Criteria

A more insidious defect is to state a "criterion" that tells the students little or nothing that they don't already know. Consider these:

To the satisfaction of the instructor.

Must be able to make 80 percent on a multiple-choice exam.

Must pass a final exam.

Students know they have to satisfy the instructor. What *would* be news would be a description of what they have to do to produce such satisfaction. If instructors do, in fact, make judgments about whether students are or are not competent, there is no reason why those instructors cannot reveal the basis for their judgments. Of course, it might take some thought and effort. So what? That's what professional instruction is all about.

The second and third examples above tell the student a little something about the administrative aspects of the criterion situation but tell them nothing about how well they will have to do whatever the objective demands. That is, "80 percent on a multiple-choice exam" does not describe the desired quality of performance. We all know how easy it is to manipulate the difficulty of an examination by varying the wording and the choice of items. The 80 percent isn't the problem; it is the *substance* of the 80 percent that is the problem. If you were told, for example, that you were expected to be able to shoot well enough so that 80 percent of your shots fell within the bull's-eye, you would have a description of competence level that you could do something about. But to say that you had to earn 80 percent on a multiple-choice exam or 90 percent on an essay exam or that you had to reach an 80/90 criterion is to tell you little that could help you to guide your own efforts. The same is true for the designer of the instruction—such "criteria" do not help in deciding the type and amount of instruction for accomplishing the objective.

If you want to see how bad things can get, read the following, which warrants exposure but not comment:

> *Given twenty problems dealing with three operations in decimals and two types of percent and percentage problems; 90 percent of the students whose chronological ages range from 11.0 to 11.11 and who have given evidence, by the Lorge-Thorndike or other ability test, that they will achieve above the third quartile, will solve the problems and write solutions at 92 percent accuracy as evidenced by scores on a teacher-devised test administered by May (!!!!).*

To test the criterion in an objective, ask whether the criterion (1) says something about the quality of performance you desire, (2) says something about the quality of the *individual* performance rather than the group performance, and (3) says something about a real, rather than an imaginary, standard.

Related Issues

Five issues on which I would like to comment still remain. They don't have to do with the actual wording of the objectives, so they do not fall strictly within the limits of this book. But since they're common problems relating to objectives, they deserve a mention.

Irrelevant Test Items

A common bad practice is that of teaching one thing and then testing for another; that is, of using test items that ask for performance other than that called for by the objectives. Such a practice is deceitful, regardless of the rationalizations offered for its use. For example, though an objective may make it clear that students need to be able to *make change*, irrelevant test items might look like these:

1. Define money.

2. Name the President on the fifty-dollar bill.

3. Describe the risks of not being able to count.

None of these items ask the student to do what the objective asks, namely, to make change. As a result, no one will discover whether or not a student can perform as required, and no one will learn what remedial actions, if any, should be initiated. But that doesn't stop people from rationalizing this bad practice:

"They can't make change if they don't know what money is."

"They can't really appreciate money if they don't know whose faces are on the bills."

"I like to vary the type of items I use to make my tests interesting."

"I'm teaching for transfer."

"I want my tests to be a learning situation."

"Trainees should learn by discovery."

Regardless of the excuse, the use of irrelevant test items in assessing achievement of an objective poses several dangers. For one thing, it models deceit for the students. It tells them that it doesn't bother the instructor to teach one thing and then test for something else. It confirms the instructor as the enemy. For another, with irrelevant test items you will never know whether the student has learned to perform as desired. A well-written objective will prescribe the form of the test items by which the objective can be assessed.

Wrong Objectives

The charge that certain objectives are trivial is usually made for one of two reasons, neither of which has anything to do with how the objectives are worded. The triviality charge is usually aimed at objectives that look less potent than they really are and at those that are, in fact, trivial because they don't relate to anything of importance.

First, you can't tell whether an objective is trivial just by reading it; you have to compare it with the world around it— with the consequence of not achieving the objective. If it wouldn't matter to anyone or anything whether the objective was or was not accomplished, then it may indeed be trivial. If, on the other hand, some significant consequence would result from non-accomplishment of the objective, then it isn't trivial, regardless of how simply it may be worded or how "small" the performance described is.

For example, suppose an objective for a bank teller says, "Be able to smile visibly when serving a customer." That sounds pretty Mickey Mouse until you learn that grouchy tellers lose customers and sometimes lose their jobs. There's nothing trivial about losing customers, and there's certainly nothing trivial about losing your job.

Another example: An objective for bartenders says, "Be able to serve customers without spilling or slamming." (They're supposed to be able to serve without slamming bottles or glasses on the bar or table.) Now you've got to admit that sounds pretty trivial as an objective. But when compared to the consequences of not accomplishing the objective, a different picture emerges. In this particular hotel chain, bartenders who slam glasses or spill drinks on customers are fired. Is that trivial? So objectives that lead to meaningful consequences are not trivial, regardless of how they may sound to the casual reader.

Objectives are also charged with triviality when they are incorrectly derived. Objectives ought to come from somewhere to serve meaningful, rather than merely cosmetic, purposes. Suppose you're visiting your brother Flatson at the school where he teaches, and this conversation takes place:

You: Hi, Flat. What are you up to?

Flat: You wouldn't believe it! I've got to trump up a bunch of #*$*&^ objectives.

You: What in the world *for?*

Flat: Oh, the principal just came by and ordered us to write objectives for all of our courses. Said that the new district policy requires everybody to have objectives.

You: So where are you getting these objectives?

Flat: Heck, I'm just writing some to describe what I'm already doing in my courses.

Unfortunately, this scene has been played out in too many school districts and corporate training departments. As I said, objectives ought to come from somewhere if they are to be worth drafting, and writing them to reflect existing instruction is putting the cart before the horse. Why bother to construct blueprints after the house is built, other than for cosmetic reasons intended to convince someone that you constructed your instruction in a rational manner? (For information about how to derive objectives in a systematic manner, review Part III in *Making Instruction Work,* by R. F. Mager.)

False Taxonomizing

A taxonomy is a way of classifying things according to their relationships. If you have never heard the term before, you should skip this section, as it does not describe a problem that relates to you. You won't miss a thing.

Every now and again we bump into someone who claims to be having unusual difficulty in drafting objectives. They feel their objectives are unsatisfactory, even though review of their work reveals objectives that are quite well stated. Then why the discomfort? Taxonomitis. For some reason these troubled souls are trying to distort their objectives to fit some sort of taxonomy (classification system). Just because it is *possible* to write objectives that reflect different levels of a classification scheme, they seem to feel it is therefore *necessary* to do so. "All our objectives are at the same taxonomy level," they complain. "We need some at other levels," they assert. One person even felt that objectives had to conform to a normal distribution of classification levels to be considered satisfactory. What in the world for? I don't know where such an idea originated, but I wish it would go away.

If you have derived your objectives from a real need and have described what you want your students to be able to do, why change the objectives just to conform to a taxonomy?

Now, a taxonomy, or classification scheme, can be useful in reminding you of the range of objectives you might write or select, the words you might use in describing your intents, or the kinds of test items that might be appropriate for assessing your objectives. But to deliberately write objectives to fit a classification system rather than a need seems a gross misuse of these thinking tools.

Orphan Objectives

One of the strangest and most wasteful practices in relation to objectives is that of writing some and then putting them on the shelf—unused. People who engage in this ritual then complain bitterly that objective writing is a waste of time. And for them it is. If they don't know what to do with objectives once they have them, or if they don't intend to find out what to do with them, then they are clearly wasting their time in writing them.

Why would anyone write objectives who didn't intend to do something with them? Mostly because some well-meaning administrator or manager ordered them to. But to order people to write objectives without making sure they know *how*, and *why*, is to invite dissension and frustration. After all, drafting objectives is only one of a series of steps in the analysis, design, and implementation of instruction. To order that it be carried out in a vacuum is a wasteful practice; at the very least, it will produce objectives that do little more than gather dust.

"Attitude" Objectives

Sometimes you will see statements like the following:

Be able to appreciate the importance of customer service.

Have a favorable attitude toward reading.

Develop a positive attitude toward safety.

Have an appreciation for literature.

Have a professional attitude.

Where is the performance? There isn't any. Therefore *they aren't objectives.* They are not specific descriptions of intent. Statements like these describe *states of being;* they do not describe *doing.* While such statements may address areas of extreme importance, it is misleading to refer to them as "attitude" or "affective" *objectives.*

The risk in doing so is that the readers of such statements may be lulled into thinking these are objectives merely because the topics are important; and objective writers may be lulled into thinking that when they have written such statements, they have finished their work. On the contrary, they have just begun. You see, statements about the affective (feeling, attitude) are *always* statements of *inference,* not of performance. They are predictions about future behavior that are inferred from the circumstantial evidence of what people say and do. Thus, if you see me stuffing myself with popcorn, you might infer that I have a favorable attitude toward popcorn and will eat popcorn when the opportunity presents itself. You may or may not be correct, but the behavior is the only basis you have for the inference.

If we're serious about accomplishing one or more of our affective and other abstract intentions, how, then, can we describe them in the form of objectives? We perform a goal analysis. Here's how.

1. Derive the performances that would satisfy you that the intent had been achieved.

2. Write a complete sentence to describe each of the performances.

3. Check-mark those performances that are already in the repertoire of your target audience. In other words, mark the ones your target people already know how to do.

4. Write an objective describing each of the performances left
    unchecked during the previous step. (You need write objec-
    tives for only these items, because these are the only ones
    you'll need to teach. The remaining performances will be
    included in your list of expectations but won't need to be
    turned into complete objectives.)

Here's a quick example. A manager was concerned that
employees "be safety conscious." But what did that mean? How
would he recognize someone who was acceptably safety conscious? Clearly, his first step was to say what he meant by "safety conscious" in terms of performance before he could find
out (a) how many people already met the expectations and
(b) what he would have to do to get the rest of the people to
meet the expectations.

After some thought, the manager decided that people who
were safety conscious:

a. Wear their safety equipment when appropriate.

b. Follow safety rules at all times.

c. Report safety hazards to the proper person(s).

Once the meaning of "safety conscious" was described in
terms of expected human performances, it was easy to decide
what to do next. He quickly determined that everybody
already knew how to do the second and third items listed
above, but some didn't know the proper way to put on and/or
use some of the safety equipment. To accomplish his goal,
then, the manager needed only to write one or more objectives
describing the expectations regarding safety equipment and to
arrange instruction for those who could not yet perform to the
objectives' criteria.

Note that the objectives were written to describe the performances rather than the abstract state (safety consciousness) they represented as it would have been useless to describe the intent in such vague terms as these:

Be able to demonstrate safety consciousness in all appropriate situations.

That isn't an objective as it includes no DOING word. The words "be able to" don't turn gibberish into objectives.

Whenever you need to write objectives to describe states or conditions that are essentially abstract (understanding, knowing, attitude, motivation, feeling, appreciation), first use the goal analysis or similar procedure to help define those abstractions in terms of the performances that would represent their accomplishment. Once you've done that, you'll be in a position to decide which of those performances you'll have to teach, i.e., the things that your trainees cannot already do.

(Hmm. If statements about abstract states such as attitudes can't be called objectives until the performances which define them have been derived and described, wouldn't it be fair to say that there's no such thing as an "affective" objective?)

The checklist on page 166 can help you review your draft objectives. But try not to be constrained by form and format. State what you want your students to be able to do, what they will be doing it with or without, and how well they will have to do it for you to consider them competent.

And now, what's your pleasure?

A little more practice wouldn't hurt.   **Turn to page 155.**

I'm ready to test my skill.   **Turn to page 173.**

9
Sharpen Your Skill

The old saw about practice making perfect has about as much truth in it as the one about experience being the best teacher. Practice will improve a skill, and experience can improve one's competence—but *only* if there is feedback regarding the quality of the performance. If you don't find out how well you are doing while you are practicing or experiencing, your skill is not likely to improve. Therefore, while practice is important, practice with feedback is essential if the practice is to serve its purpose. Which may be the long way around the barn to tell you that this short chapter offers some guided practice in recognizing useful characteristics of objectives and a wee bit of practice in editing a few that are in need of repair.

"Wait a minnit," I hear you saying. "How come the objective of the book wants me to be able to *recognize* useful characteristics and now you want me to do a *repair* job?" Good question. Answer: This is a practice chapter to help you sharpen your discrimination skill. Asking you to repair a few objectives will cause you to pay closer attention to what you are learning to discriminate.

So sharpen your pencil and have at it.

Practice Items

Read the statements below. Place a check mark in the appropriate column to the right if a statement includes a performance, conditions under which the performance is to appear, and/or a criterion by which successful performance of the objective can be assessed.

HINT: Always begin decoding an objective by circling the performance. If no performance is stated, it isn't an objective and you need go no further.

	PERFORMANCE	CONDITIONS	CRITERION
1. When you complete this section, you will know the history of money as a medium of exchange.	___	___	___
2. Without references, be able to describe (write) the key conditions that promote learning and those that retard or interfere with learning.	___	___	___
3. On a live patient undergoing laparoscopy, be able to locate (point to) the following structures: ovary, ligaments of the ovary, fallopian tube, uterus.	___	___	___
4. Given twenty minutes of instruction and a lab exercise, be able to develop an understanding of the difference between igneous, metamorphic, and sedimentary rocks. Criterion: 80% correct.	___	___	___
5. Given a progressive discipline situation (where an unjustifiable lack of performance improvement follows the initial corrective discussion), be able to conduct a progressive discipline discussion using the key actions listed in the PDS Discussion Guide.	___	___	___

Turn to page 158.

	PERFORMANCE	CONDITIONS	CRITERION

1. When you complete this section, you will know the history of money as a medium of exchange. ___ ___ ___

2. Without references, be able to describe (write) the key conditions that promote learning and those that retard or interfere with learning. ✓ ✓ ✓

3. On a live patient undergoing laparoscopy, be able to locate (point to) the following structures: ovary, ligaments of the ovary, fallopian tube, uterus. ✓ ✓ ✓

Comments

1. This statement is pretty much useless as a statement of intended outcome. For one thing, it doesn't state a performance ("knowing" might be a state of mind, but it isn't a performance).

   You didn't get caught on the false given (condition), did you? "When you complete this section" tells you something about the learning experience; it doesn't describe a condition that will affect the desired (unstated) performance.

   Finally, no criterion is stated—or even implied.

   Statements such as these may be useful as course descriptions, but they should not be confused with objectives.

2. Here a performance (describing) and an indicator behavior (writing) are both stated, providing good information about what someone will be expected to be able to do.

   "Without references" is the conditon stated. Performing without references would be different from performing with references available.

   A criterion is implied rather than clearly stated. We are told that we must describe conditions (whatever they are), but we aren't told anything about the quality of the expected performance. This objective could be improved by a clearer description of the criterion.

3. Here again, both a covert performance (locate) and suitable indicator (point to) are stated. The key condition, "On a live patient," is also described.

   In this objective, a criterion is clearly implied. The objective says to be able to locate four specified items. If less than the four are located, the objective hasn't yet been achieved. (If you disagree, don't argue—fix the objective.)

	PERFORMANCE	CONDITIONS	CRITERION
4. Given twenty minutes of instruction and a lab exercise, be able to develop an understanding of the difference between igneous, metamorphic, and sedimentary rocks. Criterion: 80% correct.	____	____	____
5. (Note: The following objective is intended for managers.) Given a progressive discipline situation (where an unjustifiable lack of performance improvement follows the initial corrective discussion) be able to conduct a progressive discipline discussion using the key actions listed in the PDS Discussion Guide.	✓	✓	____

4. You didn't get caught on this false given, did you? It describes instructional procedure; it does *not* describe the conditions under which the performance is to occur. No performance is stated. And if it isn't, what possible meaning could there be to saying "80% correct"? It's rather like saying "Be able to understand the problems of the world. Criterion: 80% correct." Just labeling something a criterion doesn't make it one.

5. The performance is clearly stated (. . . be able to conduct a progressive discipline discussion . . .).

   Two conditions are also clearly stated (even though we may not have the background to understand the meaning of the first one). The first is "Given a progressive discipline situation . . . ," and the second is "using the key actions listed in the PDS Discussion Guide."

   The second item should be thought of as a condition rather than as a criterion. Why? Because it tells us something about what we will be doing during our performance, i.e., using the key actions in the Discussion Guide, but it doesn't tell us what to look for to decide whether the performance meets the intended standards. This objective would be a lot easier to read if it were cast in the form:

   Performance: Conduct a progressive discipline discussion.

   Givens: PDS Discussion Guide.
               Progressive discipline situation (where an unjustifiable lack of performance improvement follows the initial corrective discussion)

   Criterion: (missing)

Turn to page 163.

Practice Items

Try a few more. If a statement includes a performance, conditions, and/or a criterion, place a check mark in the appropriate column to its right.

	PERFORMANCE	CONDITIONS	CRITERION
1. The student will learn the basic sanitary standards in the food industry, according to local and state codes.	____	____	____
2. Students will gain knowledge of the structure of the molecule and briefly describe how the structures can be demonstrated.	____	____	____
3. <u>Given:</u> A need or assignment to conduct a performance appraisal, appropriate forms, and an interviewee, <u>Performance:</u> Conduct an appraisal interview. <u>Criteria:</u> Interviewee reports satisfaction with the discussion and states an intent to achieve the agreed-on work targets for the upcoming period. The interviewer and interviewee are willing to sign the form as accurate.	____	____	____
4. <u>Condition:</u> A three-hour discussion of the merits of a flat tax. <u>Performance:</u> Present (verbally) the advantages and disadvantages of a flat-tax system. <u>Criterion:</u> 90% accuracy.	____	____	____
5. <u>Given:</u> A functioning Meltdown Six computer terminal, be able to log on and send a message of your choice to any specified address. <u>Criterion:</u> All messages are received by their addressees.	____	____	____

Turn to Page 164.

	PERFORMANCE	CONDITIONS	CRITERION

1. The student will learn the basic sanitary standards in the food industry, according to local and state codes.

| | ___ | ___ | ___ |

2. Students will gain knowledge of the structure of the molecule and briefly (describe) how the structures can be demonstrated.

| | ✓ | ___ | ___ |

3. Given: A need or assignment to conduct a performance appraisal, appropriate forms, and an interviewee.

   Performance: (Conduct an appraisal interview.)

   Criteria: Interviewee reports satisfaction with the discussion, and states an intent to achieve the agreed-on work targets for the upcoming period. The interviewer and the interviewee are willing to sign the form as accurate.

| | ✓ | ✓ | ✓ |

4. Condition: A three-hour discussion of the merits of a flat tax.

   Performance: (Present (verbally) the advantages and disadvantages of a flat-tax system.)

   Criterion: 90% accuracy.

| | ✓ | ___ | ___ |

5. Given: A functioning Meltdown Six computer terminal, be able to (log on) and (send a message) of your choice to any specified address.

   Criterion: All messages are received by their addressees.

| | ✓ | ✓ | ✓ |

Comment

1. This is another of those nothing statements. So the student will learn. How nice. But what about the result of that learning? You haven't been let in on the secret. No performance, no need to look further.

2. Yet another nothing statement. Again, this statement might be useful as part of a course description, but is worthless as a description of an important outcome to be achieved.

3. Here is a good objective. After reading it, you know what you're expected to be able to do, the conditions under which you'll be doing it, and the criteria by which the performance will be evaluated. Use this one as a model for your own drafts.

4. Uh, oh. Here's another of those cosmetically nifty statements—nice format, but no substance.

    The item listed as a condition is merely a description of part of the instructional process, and the "criterion" isn't. Remember: Calling it a criterion doesn't necessarily make it one. In the context of this statement, "90% accuracy" has no meaning.

    About all we can say in favor of this item is that a performance is stated. True, that's more information than a lot of "objectives" provide, but not enough.

5. This is another good example, even though the performance was stated in the objective as part of the "Givens."

    Performance: Send messages to specified addresses.

    Conditions: Given a functioning computer terminal.

    Criteria: All messages get to where they're sent.

Now try your hand at fixing objectives in need of some repair.

Objectives Checklist

Your objectives will communicate better if you can answer "YES" to the following questions:

Performance

1. Is your main intent stated?

2. If the main intent is covert (mental), is an indicator behavior stated?

3. Is that indicator behavior the simplest and most direct one you can think of?

Conditions

4. Have you described what the learner will be given, or be deprived of, during performance of the objective?

5. Have you described all of the conditions that will influence the shape of the performance?

Criteria

6. Have you described how well the learner must perform to be acceptable?

7. Do those criteria describe some aspect of the performance, or the product of the performance, rather than instructional process or meaningless percentages?

8. Where a percentage is included in a criterion, does it reflect a realistic expectation?

Editing Practice

Here are some objectives in need of repair. Strike any unnecessary or confusing words, and add indicators where performances are covert (mental, cognitive). Where useful characteristics are missing, add them. If you are not familiar with the content, make something up. The checklist of the facing page may be of help. (Hint: It will be easier to rewrite these on another piece of paper or on your word processor.)

1. Given a potential customer, be able to describe the features and benefits of your product.

2. Having completed as much practice as you feel necessary, be able to type a business letter. Criterion: Satisfaction of the instructor.

3. Know how a personal pager works.

4. In a classroom environment, be able to make a five-minute presentation on a topic of your choice. The presentation should show good form.

5. After studying the text and discussing it with colleagues, identify examples of ethical and unethical conduct.

When you have finished your repairs, turn to the next page.

How'd You Do?

1. *Given a potential customer, be able to describe the features and benefits of your product.*

   This one needs only minor repair. A performance is stated, and so is one of the key conditions that would influence that performance. What's missing is a criterion that would suggest how to judge the product—describing performance.

   If you were asked to demonstrate accomplishment of this objective, however, you might have some questions about the conditions. "Wouldn't I have an actual product handy while I'm explaining features and benefits?" "If not, wouldn't I at least have some product literature to refer to?" Taking questions such as those into consideration, your objective might look like this:

   Given a potential customer, a product, and related literature, be able to describe the features and benefits of the product. Criteria: All key benefits and features highlighted in the literature must be described; all information presented must be factual; customer must not be insulted, demeaned, embarrassed, or ridiculed.

2. *Having completed as much practice as you feel necessary, be able to type a business letter. Criterion: Satisfaction of the instructor.*

   The verbiage before the comma represents a false given; it talks about instructional practice rather than about conditions that would affect the performance of typing a letter. Add the conditions under which the typing is expected to occur. On a 1912 Remington typewriter? Using a computer keyboard?

   The performance is fine, but the "criterion" stinks. We already know that we need to satisfy the instructor. So those words tell us nothing. What would be useful would be to learn just *what* would satisfy the instructor. A box of candy? A case of beer? Here's one way to re-write this objective:

Given a legible handwritten letter and a functioning computer, be able to type the letter in accordance with the standards described in Manual 12-21.

3. *Know how a personal pager works.*

   This objective states no performance, no conditions, and no criteria, so fixing it will require more crystal-balling on your part. What is "know" supposed to mean in this context? Be able to describe what a pager does? Trace the signal flow through the circuits? Describe the theory of pagers? What? You'll have to decide. (Remember: When someone asks you to deal with "fuzzies" such as these, they abdicate to you the power to decide what they mean. Take advantage of it.) I arbitrarily decided that the objective-writer wants me to be able to repair pagers, and so modified the statement this way:

   Given all necessary tools, spare parts, and reference materials, be able to repair any brand of pager. The repaired device must function to manufacturer specifications described in the Service Manual.

   Your objective will look different, of course, depending on what meaning you decided to select.

4. *In a classroom environment, be able to make a five-minute presentation on a topic of your choice. The presentation should show good form.*

   Hooray! An objective with a nicely stated performance . . . but that's about all. Is "in a classroom environment . . ." a condition or a description of the place where the practicing will occur? If the objective-writer intends for us to learn to make presentations in classrooms only, then the words before the comma are a condition. If the intent is for us to make presentations in other environments as well, the words before the comma should be deleted.

The only words that smell like a criterion here are "The presentation should show good form." But what does "good form" mean? Standing up straight, chin in, chest out, tummy sucked in? Fingers extended and joined? What? This is clearly an instance where the objective-writer should have completed a goal analysis on this "fuzzy" before inflicting it on us to divine its meaning. To fix this statement, you'll have to decide what "good form" means and add any conditions you think are relevant to the performance. Here's one possibility:

Given visuals of your choice and a topic of your choice, be able to make a five-minute presentation. Criteria:

a. *Didn't turn back to audience,*

b. *Wrote legibly when using flip chart or board,*

c. *Removed visuals from view when not in use, and*

d. *Used gestures and movement to emphasize points made.*

It's anybody's guess what the objective-writer meant by "good form," so almost any definition you used would be appropriate, so long as it is described as clearly as possible and is written down.

5. *After studying the text and discussing it with colleagues, iden-tify examples of ethical and unethical conduct.*

Things are getting stickier. In dealing with this one, it would help to know from which course the objective was taken; it was swiped from a nursing course. At least that helps pinpoint the subject.

The first problem here, of course, is that the words before the comma describe instructional procedures rather than an outcome. Delete them. The second problem is that we don't know which of the several possible meanings of "identify" is intended. Add an indicator behavior. Finally, there is no criterion. One needs to be added.

To fix this objective, it helps to ask the question, "Now how could I find out whether a practicing nurse can identify ethical and unethical nursing behavior?" Here's one way to do it.

Given videotaped scenes depicting a nurse carrying out various duties, be able to identify (describe) instances of unethical behavior. Criterion: All instances of unethical behavior (as defined by the NP Ethical Handbook) are described.

10
Self-Test

On the following pages is a short skill check with which you can check your skill at discriminating (pointing to) the characteristics of objectives. Answer all the questions, and then check your responses on pages 176–179.

The self-test consists of twenty items. In the first ten, you are asked whether or not each statement contains a performance. In the last ten, you will need to make three discriminations for each item (whether or not it contains a performance; whether or not it contains a condition; and whether or not it contains a criterion). If you make no more than one error in the first ten items and no more than six errors in the next ten, color yourself competent. Otherwise, you may want to review the chapter(s) dealing with the characteristic(s) on which we disagree.

Notice that a perfect score is not expected. Why not? Because you may not be familiar with the content of some of the objectives. In such cases it may be difficult to recognize conditions or criteria that aren't clearly labeled as such.

Have at it!

SELF-TEST

A. Do the following statements include performances? Does each at least tell what the learner will be doing when demonstrating achievement of the objective?

	States a Performance	
	YES	NO
1. Understand the principles of power grids.	____	____
2. Be able to write correct examples of the logical fallacy of the undistributed middle.	____	____
3. Internalize the meaning of Ohm's Law.	____	____
4. Without the use of memory aids, be able to name the bones of the body.	____	____
5. Know the needs for nursing care associated with the stresses of life situations and with common aspects of illness.	____	____
6. Demonstrate a *deep* understanding of the plays of Shakespeare.	____	____
7. Be able to identify *(circle)* objectives that include a statement of desired performance.	____	____
8. Develop an ability to recognize that the practical application of democratic ideals requires time, adjustment, and continuous effort.	____	____
9. Appreciate the ability of others, and perform as an intelligent spectator.	____	____
10. Be able to describe the log-on procedure for your own computer.	____	____

B. Read the statements below. Place a check mark in the appropriate column to indicate any characteristic of a useful objective you find in each.

	PERFORMANCE	CONDITIONS	CRITERION

11. Without memory aids or other assistance, demonstrate a knowledge of the rules of grammar.

12. Be able to write an essay on evolution.

13. Using any reference materials, be able to name correctly every item shown on each of twenty blueprints.

14. Be able to write a description of the steps involved in making a blueprint.

15. On the 25-yard range, be able to draw your service revolver and fire five rounds from the hip within three seconds. At 25 yards, all rounds must hit the standard silhouette target.

16. Be able to know well the cardinal rules of good manners.

17. Given an oral description of the events involved in an accident, be able to fill out a standard accident report.

18. Be able to write a coherent essay on the subject "How to Write Objectives for a Course in Law Appreciation." Course notes may be used, as well as any references.

19. Be able to develop logical approaches in the solution of personnel problems.

20. Without reference materials, be able to describe three common points of view regarding racial inferiority or superiority that are not supported by available research.

Solutions for Part A

Performances are circled.

	States a Performance	
	YES	NO
1. Understand the principles of power grids.		✓
2. Be able to (write) correct examples of the logical fallacy of the undistributed middle.	✓	
3. Internalize the meaning of Ohm's Law.		✓
4. Without the use of memory aids, be able to (name) the bones of the body.	✓	
5. Know the needs for nursing care associated with the stresses of life situations and with common aspects of illness.		✓
6. Demonstrate a *deep* understanding of the plays of Shakespeare.		✓
7. Be able to (identify (circle)) objectives that include a statement of desired performance.	✓	
8. Develop an ability to recognize that the practical application of democratic ideals requires time, adjustment, and continuous effort.		✓
9. Appreciate the ability of others, and perform as an intelligent spectator.		✓
10. Be able to (describe) the log-on procedure for your own computer.	✓	

Comments for Part A

1. A goal analysis would be in order here to determine the meaning of "understand."

2. You can tell whether someone is writing, so it qualifies as a performance.

3. Same problem as with Item 1.

4. Naming is a performance; you can tell when it is being done.

5. Same problem as with Item 1. An important goal, perhaps, but no performance is stated.

6. Underlining doesn't make words more specific—and that's <u>really true.</u>

7. Identifying is a covert performance that can be directly assessed by a single indicator behavior such as circling, underlining, or checking.

8. Again, perhaps an important thought, but what would you be doing when recognizing that application of ideals requires time?

9. You didn't get caught on the "perform as an intelligent spectator" part of this, did you? What would you be doing when performing? Shouting? Throwing bottles at an umpire? Sitting quietly? We are given nary a clue.

10. Describing is a performance. We are not told whether the describing must be oral or in writing, but either way the describing is a performance.

Solutions for Part B

Performances are circled.
Conditions are underlined.
Criteria are in italics.

	PERFORMANCE	CONDITIONS	CRITERION
11. <u>Without memory aids or other assistance,</u> demonstrate a knowledge of the rules of grammar.		✓	
12. Be able to (write) an essay on evolution.	✓		
13. <u>Using any reference materials,</u> be able to (name) *correctly every item shown on each of twenty blueprints.*	✓	✓	✓
14. Be able to (write) a description of the steps involved in making a blueprint.	✓		
15. <u>On the 25-yard range,</u> be able to (draw) your <u>service revolver</u> and (fire five rounds from the hip) <u>within three seconds.</u> *At 25 yards, all rounds must hit the standard silhouette target.*	✓	✓	✓
16. Be able to know *well* the cardinal rules of good manners.			
17. <u>Given an oral description of the events involved in an accident,</u> be able to (fill out) a standard accident report.	✓	✓	
18. Be able to (write) a coherent essay on the subject "How to Write Objectives for a Course in Law Appreciation." <u>Course notes may be used, as well as any references.</u>	✓	✓	
19. Be able to develop logical approaches in the solution of personnel problems.			
20. <u>Without reference materials,</u> be able to (describe) *three common points* of view regarding racial inferiority or superiority that are *not supported by available research.*	✓	✓	✓

Comments for Part B

11. *Demonstrate* is that trap word that often leads us to believe we are saying something specific.

12. Though you may read an implication that the writing must be done without reference materials, that condition is not stated. Neither are we told how the essay will be judged competent.

13. This one says something about performance, conditions, and criterion. It may be an objective that would appear at the bottom of an objectives hierarchy—that is, it may be a very low-level skill—but it is an objective.

14. Here you may feel that a criterion is implied. It says to write the steps, and that could be read to mean "write all the steps correctly." And then, again, it might mean something else. If a few words will make the criterion clear, it is better to add them than to rely on inferences.

15. You may not agree with the purpose of the statement, but it is a good objective.

16. Italicizing *doesn't* make it so—or specific.

17. Again, you may read an implication of "without error." I wouldn't, because I never assume that perfection is demanded unless it is explicitly specified. Perfection is seldom a realistic expectation.

18. What does coherent mean? How would we recognize coherence if we saw it? We are not told.

19. Ah, well. Another nice-sounding statement, but not an objective. Besides, the word "develop" usually means that the statement is talking about the process of acquiring the intended competence, rather than about the result of the acquiring.

20. This one is tricky. How well must the describing be done? Well, it has to describe three points of view not supported by research. Not much of a criterion, I'll admit, but a start.

Scoring

To compare your responses against the criterion, do the following:

1. In items 1 through 10, circle every incorrect check mark.

2. In items 11 through 20, circle any space that you left empty but that should have a check mark. Circle the spaces you checked that you should have left empty.

3. Total the circled spaces (errors). If there are seven or fewer, AND if they include no more than one error in recognizing the presence or absence of a performance, consider yourself competent to recognize the presence or absence of the characteristics of a useful objective.

If you have more errors than specified in the criterion, you may want to review the chapter(s) dealing with the characteristic(s) on which we disagree.

NOTE: When there is disagreement about the meaning of an objective, it is always faster and easier to fix it than argue about it.

One final thought.
You are now ready to begin
drafting your own objectives.
May you be as picky with *them*
as you have been with mine.

The Stoner
and the Stonees

Professor, professor," cried the second-assistant digger-upper. "I think I've found something."

"Oh," replied the professor, raising his archeological head from the archeological dirt. "What is it?"

"It's a large stone with writing on it," enthused the excited assistant. "Maybe it's another part of the *Great Recipe of Life.*"

"Let me see," said the professor as he raised his magnificent magnifying glass. "No, no, I think you're mistaken. See these markings? These are the names of people."

"People?" queried the assistant. "What people?"

"Hmm," replied the great one, profoundly. "It looks as though these are the names of people who contributed to the shaping and the fixing of a book."

"Why would anyone put their names in stone?" asked the assistant.

"Well," replied the professor, "it says here that the author didn't want anyone to forget just who it was that beat and bashed his words into presentable shape. He wanted the world to remember each and every one for what they did to his work."

"What did they do to it?" asked the assistant, edging closer for a better look.

"A number of things, according to these hieroglyphics. For example, it says here that Dave Cram, Margo Hicks, and John Warriner had something to do with making sure the manuscript hung together. Continuity check is the term he used.

"Then he lists some people who helped test to make sure the book accomplished what it was supposed to. He called that his outcome check. The names are Maryjane Rees, John Alston, Joe de Hazes, Jeannette Hanne, Grant Bodwell, Michael Hanau, Jerry Tuller, and Jean White.

"After that he lists those who participated in a . . . an attitude check, apparently to make sure the book didn't contain any accidental turnoffs. Their names are Billy Koscheski, Elizabeth Epperson, Pauline Stone, Ann Redl, Dick Niedrich, Andy Stevens, Jane Kilkenny, and Marilyn McElhaney.

"Diane Pope is mentioned in deeply chiseled letters because she contributed a special example. Jeanne Mager is named as chief chiseler."

"Look at this!" cried the assistant. "Here are some words with a box chiseled around them. What do they say?"

"These," continued the professor as he tried to push his nose through his magnifying glass, "are the names of those who helped to test the cover design of the book. They are Frank Sedei, John Gray, Karen Schwartz, Sue Markle, Jim Straubel, Mike Nisos, Roger Kaufman, Margo Hicks, Bob Morgan, Al Collins, Joan Fleetwood, Stephen Daeschner, Bob Reichart, Harold Stolovitch, Wally Stauffer, and Jan Kaufman.

"And," continued the professor pomporiously, "here is a clump of names of those who tested other cover designs. Looks like Clair Miller, Bill Valen, Dan Piskorik, Letitia Wiley, Carol Valen, Eileen Mager, Johan Adriaanse, Bob White, Jim Reed, Ethel Robinson, Fahad Omair, Phil Postel, Gérard

Conesa, David Heath, and Paul Guersch."

"That's amazing!" wowed the assistant.

"Help me topple this big boulder! We must leave no stone unturned." Which they did.

"Aha!" amazed the professor. "There are even more names here. Look. These are people who helped shape the third edition."

"What did they do?" queried the assistant.

"Several things. Good and bad samples from their vintage objectives collections were generously offered by Paul Whitmore, Richard Lookatch, Kay Newell, Ann Parkman, Ken Fackler, and James T. McGoldrick.

"Initial trampling was kindly undertaken by that virtuoso manuscript bashist, David Cram. Following the revision, another group of miscreants gleefully added their footprints: Carl Winkelbauer, Al Wilson, Marianne Hoffman, Hilton Goldman, Jerri Shold, Ann D. Demonet, John R. Criswell, Diane Wardrop, Lee Alderman, Wayne Seamans, and Eileen Mager."

"Gee whiz," exhaled the assistant. "That author didn't seem to know how to do anything by himself."

"Perhaps not," was the reply. "But it says here—you see these large chiselings—it says that those who would do unto others should care what those others prefer. That's why these people were asked to try on the manuscript. They helped to make it communicate better . . . and that's why they were stoned."

Index